KINGDOM PEACES

A DEVOTIONAL OF MUSINGS, MEANDERINGS & MEDITATIONS

TAMELA L. WINFREY

KINGDOM PEACES
A DEVOTIONAL OF MUSINGS, MEANDERINGS & MEDITATIONS

Copyright © 2022
Evangelist Tamela L. Winfrey, Author
Contact the Author: authortamelawinfrey16@gmail.com

All rights reserved. No part of this book may be reproduced, stored in a retrieved system, or transmitted in any form or any means, electronic, mechanical, photocopying, recording, scanning, or otherwise, without the prior written permission of the author.

DISCLAIMER
Please note that the title, "**KINGDOM PEACES**" is intentional and is not a misspelling nor is it in error. It is artistic interpretation of the primary premise of this literary work.

While every attempt has been made to provide information that is both accurate and effective, the author does not assume any responsibility for the accuracy or use/misuse of this information.

Printed in the United States of America.
ISBN 978-1955127233

Introduction

"KINGDOM PEACES"

A Devotional of Musings, Meanderings & Meditations

"Kingdom Peaces" is a unique work of art that was birthed from the essence of 'my spiritual vision' with that third eye that comedians make mention of. "Kingdom Peaces" exemplifies an aspect of transitioning from 'peace to peace.' The Word of GOD speaks of believers going from 'faith to faith', 'glory to glory', even 'strength to strength.' My prayer is that each of these "Peaces" will touch a core within the reader that has been tucked away silently...internally hemorrhaging... some of which have withered and died... some have remained mute when their inner voice cried for resurrection.

In life we have experiences that have left us wounded, battered, tattered, and torn, yet most of our upbringing commands us to press. Press... how so? Some press play, some press rewind, some press pause, but the press hasn't always addressed the root of the musing. The pull doesn't reach the cracks or the crevices as you continue to meander through life accumulating even more baggage today than yesterday. The push to survive weighs heavy as anxiety overwhelms your consciousness and prevents your attempts to meditate for clarity and revelation. "Kingdom Peaces" may just be the scalpel that opens that scar up and empowers you to stand in your truth...released and whole.

"Kingdom Peaces" is a devotional saturated with the 'Irrevocable Word of GOD.' It has purpose with 'Musings' to provoke you to jot down 'Peaces' that struck a chord. 'Meanderings' is a safe place to allow the triggers to be credited & researched with intensity as you wander down memory lane. "Kingdom Peaces" gives space for 'Meditations' that enable you to sit at HIS feet and cast your cares before HIM...a habitation that you present yourself to ELOHIM and allow HIM to minister to your desolate places. May you find power, might and strength as the inner warrior spirit is awakened as you delve into the depths of "Kingdom Peaces." May HIS 'Peaces' edify, exhort and extol your indwelling spirit for the glory of the MOST HIGH.

Acknowledgements

First, I give all the honor, glory and all the praises to *Elohim*, my *Creator*, *El Shaddai*, my blesser, and *Adonai*, my unchanging *God* for blessing me above, beyond, and exceeding my vivid imagination!!! Thank *You*, *Abba Father* for the gift of *Jesus Christ* and the gift of the HOLY SPIRIT that led me on this emotional journey. Thank *You* for the divine connections that led me to this specific space, this anointed time and place in my life. My prayer is that "KINGDOM PEACES" will be that gift to someone that is in a space where they don't know what to do and these "Peaces" will inspire them to move beyond that uncomfortable place.

I honor my Mama and my Daddy, Dot and Mann Winfrey for being faithful in the task that *Abba Father* set before them. I am grateful for the seeds that they sowed which enabled the fruition of my first literary baby. Their love and devotion to their family, not just their core, but extended family laid an unforgettable foundation to not just my siblings and me, but to so many more. I am so grateful for all that we endured because we did it as *God* ordained, as a family. Though they are not here physically to celebrate this victory for the *Kingdom of God* with me, they will always be with me, and I will always keep their memory alive. Every victory I attain for *Elohim*, is a victory for them! Mama and Daddy... We Did It!!!

#TeamDotnMannzCrew

Thank you to my babies: Khenedye J. & Kherynton J! My beloveds! My girl and my boy... *God* did just what I asked and *I am* #TeamGladAboutIt. Greater works in *Christ*! Fasten your seatbelts!!!

Thank you to my brothers and my sister: Clyde Jr, Stephany and James Sr. For those that know us: Teddy, Stephany and Smurf... that's how we roll! From Young Street to all around the world... it's *us* against everything! I love each of you for all that you do and how you stand with me without hesitation. I know that you have me and I have you! That's what Mama & Daddy taught us in that old house on Young St. If they rockin', you can bet that I'm rollin'!!!! No matter!

Honorable mention to my grandparents: Fred and Ina M. Winfrey and Earl and Lorena Moore. *My four corners*, I love and miss them! Their love and wisdom continue to illuminate my path!

I have truly been blessed on this journey to be connected with dynamic people. I have been with some since forever and I am grateful that we hung on in there. I humbly 'Thank each of you for all that you have spoken into me on this literary trek.' I have so many, so give me grace as I give 'special shout-outs!' First, I give honor to my Pastor, Dr. Sharon R. Nesbitt of Dominion World Ministries. *I am* so humbled to be a member of such an amazing Kingdom Building ministry! The teaching I have received under this 'vessel of *God*' has built me up, empowered me and provoked me to move from places of hurt and stagnation; to walk boldly as an heir of the *Most High*! I praise *Elohim* for you Apostle! May *Abba* continue to enhance your anointing to magnanimous heights. May *He* continue to extraordinarily enlarge your territory as you lead *His* remnant to the intended green pastures of *His* greatness. I want to 'thank' Evangelist Renita Hoof for her encouragement and inspiring words and prophecies. Your coaching pushed me through an open door. Thank you so much! She is a gem of a WOG for real, for real. Thank you, Renita! My friend and my sister in *Christ*, WOG Lois Hopkins! Wow! This lady has been my ear throughout this process. Anytime I called, she was always ready to listen, she always made time.

She is a faithful gatekeeper. Thank you WOG for your endless encouragement and your honest reception of each of these authentic 'Peaces'. Your selflessness and critique has been priceless! Bless you WOG! I humbly give 'thanks' for WOG Earnestine Allen for wisdom unlimited. Her foresight and discernment of revelation has been priceless and I am eternally grateful for you being a pre-reader and giving an honest assessment. Thank you so much for everything!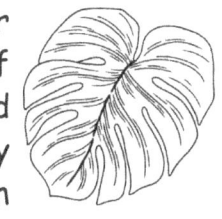

Special shout-outs: Janice Carson-Kelly, Yady Lastiri-Winfrey, Harriette Ferrell, Tracy Fair, Danielle Major, Kay Smith, Uncle Richard E. Perry, Vickie Sullivan, Glenda 'Diane' Gannaway (my mid-wife), Michael Harris, Jacqueline Hall, Amy McKinney, Tiffiney Shedd, Eva Johnson, Stephanie Young-Johnson, Sharon Golden, Tynida Davis, Donna Watson and Author Takerra Allen (my final stamp of approval). Honorable mention to The Elect Lady Ministry, Dominion World Ministries, Pastor Kent Broughton of White Springs AME (Keep Writing Prophecy) and Renita Hoof Ministries. If by chance I failed to make mention of anyone, please, please, please charge it to my head and mos def not my heart! Thank you everybody! Thank you all for being ears and some eyes to *"KINGDOM PEACES"* because it meant the world to me. Thank you for your love, loyalty and kindness! May *God* bless each of you immeasurably is my prayer!

I honor my loved ones that have transitioned because I know the cheering section would have been off the chain! This part scares me because there really are *too* many to name, but I will try to hit a few: Freddie E. Winfrey, Earlene Moore-Powell, Dorsey D. Watson, Tennessee Stevenson, Judge Winfrey, Robert 'Bob' Allen, Nora Young, Melva McKenzie, Daisy Nell Clayborn, Lousette 'G-Lou' Taylor, Alice Jeanette Gaston...

To my dearest cousin and sister, Wendy Winfrey-Tyson. Wow! This is bittersweet because I know you would be here, front and center. From eating dirt, using those blue words at 5 years old, to getting whippings for leaving that waterspout on, to riding around MoMo's house 100+ times, to walking to Aunt Ida's store 10 times a day for that penny gum, to hanging on the tree on the side of the yard, to climbing on the top of that old car sliding down the windshield... me, you and Teddy... didn't we almost have it all! I see you smiling, I hear you laughing, and I hope this makes you proud. I love you Wendy! I celebrate you in "KINGDOM PEACES" ... until we meet again! Keep watch! Love, Love, Love!

Last, but certainly not least to 'you,' whom *I* am eternally grateful to. May *God* bless the reader, the hearer and doer of *His* inexhaustible *Word*! I pray that "KINGDOM PEACES" leaves an unforgettable impact of encouragement as was the intent of its' origination. Blessings to one! Blessings to all! May you be enriched with revelation, release and renewal upon the undertaking of receiving *His* spirit which saturates this vessel from cover to cover. Blessings and honor to you!

#KINGDOMPEACES   #HISVessel   #HISWord

A Tribute to Mama "Dot"

I'd like to pay tribute to my mother, Dot Winfrey. She was the lifeline to four babies. She was a portal that **God** used to bring love into the earth. My mama's light was so bright; her love was subtle yet powerful. I still feel the warmth from the reflection that she housed. I look at my siblings, and my heart fills with joy because we strive to love as we were raised by teaching as well as by example.

The **Lord** called my mama home many years ago and in that season of despair—a season that I cried and felt life was so unfair—never fathoming that those floodgates were watering seeds that had been planted in me all of my life. I am grateful for the witness that anything is possible in **God** because those tears, that heartbreak, is poured into "Kingdom Peaces." I honor my mama because she raised her children under the admonition of the **Most High**. She was a lady at all times—her carriage was impeccable, and the legacy that I stand on always leads me back to her as a role model.

She was loving, kind, compassionate, and she loved the **Lord**. She taught me strength, courage, and resilience. She taught me how to forgive even when it isn't warranted. It took many years for that flower to blossom; but once she dropped that seed, as a true Gardener, she never fretted because she knew that good seeds birth the most beautiful and vibrant flowers. Those seeds may not blossom in a week, in a month, or even in a year, but the **Lord** promised a harvest if you faint not, and she never doubted **His** Word nor **His Power**.

This lady became a mother and a wife at a young age. She took on her role with dedication. There were days of lack, but she worked and spoke of who she put her trust in, the *living and true God*. She prayed. She stayed. She built her family on the **Cornerstone** of which she knew would never crumble. She persevered; when life gave her a bad hand of cards; she held them close because of the limitless possibilities of the **Most High**.

She was a woman of faith. My Mama was a prayer warrior. I watched her go back to school with four kids and a husband. She was pulled in so many directions; yet her tenacity and trust in the **Lord** prevailed. I saw her struggle, but I admired her because she did what she always wanted to do, become a nurse. She was excellent at her craft; she walked seamlessly in her anointing.

I remember her first year of nursing—she and a fellow nurse that had more experience were recognized for the excellency of their care. She was in the newspaper because she worked with humility and respect, and healing oil was in her hands and as she bestowed grace to her patients who were in a vulnerable position. My Mama was diligent in her mission to aid the sick.

I witnessed it when she and my daddy built a house from the ground up with four children. They weren't making a lot of money, but they stood together and again accomplished something that seemed impossible.

I remember this lady tarrying for change regarding family issues, and she would come out of her room, and many times, the manifestation was immediate; such was her faith. She loved her family.

She was a beautiful lady inside and out. Her absence has left a giant hole in the fabric of our family, but her love, her life, her light has never diminished.

I pay tribute to my mama, my shero, my first best friend. My mama was a nurturer, and she taught me so many things—even when I bucked, she taught me. So Mama, each entry in "Kingdom Peaces" is dedicated to you. You did good! I love you forever! I'll see you one sweet morning!

A Tribute to Daddy "Mann"

"Kingdom Peaces" is a tribute to a 'strong man', my daddy. My grandparents called him "Mann," and trust me, he was that, and then some. My daddy was always big and strong; he was boisterous. He was a rebel, not scared of anything or anyone. I can remember as a kid seeing him always bold and fearless. He worked hard to take care of  his family. He and my mama married young, and they stuck it out. I remember him challenging his strength by picking up the back of cars. I remember my brother, my cousin, and me hanging on his arms of steel as he flexed his muscles. He was a giant to us — my vision of Samson.

When I speak of my daddy, I can't paint a picture of his perfection, for that wouldn't be true. I am so grateful that my **Heavenly Father** is so wise that **He** will turn the tide as **He** changes our perceptions. I have a picture of my daddy with a gallon jug of brown liquor, and he was all swagged out, Cool Daddy all sunk in a chair with a smirk. When I was a young girl, I didn't like that picture because all I could see were traits that weren't flattering, but as life turned upside down, and my eyes were unveiled, I saw his heart. As this formidable giant's health deteriorated, he transformed before my very eyes into a humble man, and the transformation broke my heart; it stung. Many trips have I made in taking care of "Mann" because that is what I was trained to do, who I was trained to be. I was the oldest child, and I always had a lot of responsibility as such, so I was groomed to stand.

My daddy and I didn't always have the best relationship because I was bold and fearless. The direct reflection of one can be abrasive, but with everything there are two sides of a coin. **God** is so amazing; it's astonishing to see how **He** works all things together for good. This is scripture, and it will never return void. All the things that irritated me with him, and all the things that irritated him with me — those were the characteristics that drew us closer because he knew I was going to stand and not leave him. He knew I would not abandon my post, no matter what came against me. He knew I would be there to speak on his behalf, to ask questions, to hold people accountable because he would not be mistreated on my watch. I give **God** all the glory because He reversed the curse, and I fell in love with my daddy like a little girl should.

When I think of my daddy, I always think of Samson. Big and strong, and in the blink of an eye, he was humbled. I pushed my daddy to fight for his restoration. I fought for him. I wanted him to fight more, never realizing that the strength that wasn't visible was so much more powerful than what I was pulling on him for.

He was so much stronger in the last years as he endured betrayal upon betrayal. He lost the love of his life that he never fathomed would be taken away. Then his body betrayed him, yet he fought on. Not for himself, but for those four babies that he carried on his back all of our lives. We adored my mama, but this Mann, Ina and Fred's baby boy, the 'strong man', never bowed down; he stood tall always. Just as Samson was a testament to the power of grace, of mercy, of restoration by the power of the **Most High**, my daddy was too! He transitioned as he lived, as "Mann." A Warrior who lived until he went home. My daddy's legacy lives on in his four babies, for our love song will forever play loud in our ears, in our talks, in our walks.

I pay tribute to my daddy, 'My Samson.' Cheers to you, Daddy!

My Testimony

Many people recognize that life is fleeting, especially in this day and time. The older you're blessed to live, the more you realize that your mortality does not lie in your hands. There is one that says, 'Yes' and 'No' with a resounding echo that will not be denied. *He* is all-powerful and wise. *He* knows all things, and *He* performs them to perfection; for *He* is perfect. There is no failure in *Elohim*. That sounds all well and good and worthy of all the praise. Yet there are times when you're in the heat of battle that the flesh will cry out. "Why?"

True Story. Personally, I love *Him* so because *He* doesn't disown us as *His* creation for questioning *Him*... *Elohim*, our *Creator*. Not *He* of us but we of *Him*! Wow! *He's* so gracious. I'd like to take this time to share a bit of my testimony. Too far... too long.

At one point in my life, it appeared that I was living a pretty decent life. All was well. All the marks were checked, meaning all things were falling into place; all things seemed to be in order. My life was 'seemingly' in the correct pattern.

But in the blink of an eye, hell knocked on my door. Not only did it knock on my door, it 'whooshed' in — uninvited, mind you — and tore my near-perfect world to shreds. And all I could do was watch mass destruction rain down on me as I was standing in the midst of a tornado watching the debris swirl all around me. All I could do was cry; it was happening to me.

Within a two-year span, trauma repeatedly occurred, and I was a spectator. So, bear with me as I give you a brief summation.

I had my second beloved child, and although I was married and in the same household as my spouse, I was single because I had no emotional support. My child almost died, and I was with my beloved, basically alone, standing guard for almost a month. At one point, while overseeing the care of my child, sickness tried to overtake me. Mind you, I had endured a cesarean birth, but I was unable to rest and recover because I had to stay at my post as Mama, the gatekeeper. The daily reports from the doctor fluctuated from dismal to discouraging, and every once in a while, I would receive a hopeful word. As days passed, I grew weary because the bad seemed to outweigh the good.

I felt like I was failing because I was praying fervently; yet I didn't see the healing that I sought for my beloved. I went to the *throne of grace*, and I told **Abba Father**, that I was tired of seeing my child suffer. I told **Him** that as much as I loved this child, I gave my child back to **Him**, to my **Father**, which art in Heaven. I entrusted my beloved back to the **Creator** because I knew that **His** love was so much more than I could give to my child.

I cried myself to sleep after this prayer because I didn't want to bury a child, but I didn't want to see my child continue to suffer. I loved my beloved so much that I was willing to suffer rather than continue to watch my beloved continue to suffer. The entire pregnancy I had been plagued with problems, which my doctor blew off. You see, in my spirit I was tormented with the spirit of death, but felt I was being dramatic. I didn't even know the **Holy Spirit** personally at that juncture in my life, yet; **He** was my best friend — warning me, watching over me, encouraging me, and interceding on my behalf. I am so humbled that grace and mercy cloaked me and the life of my child was spared. **God** turned it around seamlessly, and I knew beyond a shadow of a doubt... **God** did it!

Less than six months later, my best friend, my mother, died unexpectedly. My dad was the one with health issues, but it **was my loving mother that my *Heavenly Father* called home**. Devastation beyond comprehension washed over me — mind, body, and soul. I had to wrap my mind around the thought that I was alone in this cold, cruel world. The world is never as cold as the day you lose your mother. Yet I had to do what she taught me to do... press. I (along with my dad and brother) had to see to her homegoing; all the while my heart was shattered into a gazillion pieces.

Every morning I awoke with the thought... 'Not My Mama.' After the tears, I'd hear her say, 'Straighten your face up,' and I'd dry my tears as if she was standing beside me, get up, and move forward. She was the sweetest, kindest, and most loving lady — so genuine. She loved the *Lord*, so I would 'try' to find comfort in that as things went forth, knowing that she was with the *Father*.

While preparing for her funeral, so many people came to support the family. One evening, I was at my house with some of my closest family and friends when one of my spouse's favorite cousins announced in front of all these people that he was strung out on drugs. There had been whispers and I had tried to investigate, but nothing was ever  confirmed. He denied, denied, denied. When this person made this announcement, I knew this was a point where the enemy had taken his seat on a raised platform and crossed his fiery, spindly legs and lit a cigar. This devil was gloating because he had found a place to homestead — my house.

To sum it all up, I was so lost I allowed him to stay... no inkling of how to get that demon out of my house. All I knew was that 'my Mama' was gone, and I didn't know how I was going to make it.

But guess what? One day turned into two... two to three... three quickly became a week... a week a month. Time didn't stop even though my world was knocked off its axle. And in the midst of it, chaos took root, and was elevated to the nth degree. It was hell on earth in my house. About four months later, my spouse and I split up, and I didn't have much time to grieve 'my Mama' because then I became a victim of domestic abuse/stalking. I would deal with surface issues, but was never able to deal with the core of the things affecting my heart. I was so miserable because I didn't have 'my Mama' to go through this with. I kept telling myself, 'If my Mama was here, it wouldn't be so bad.'

Approximately eight months after her death, I lost my job of eleven years, my sole source of income, a month later, 'my Daddy' almost died. He was hospitalized for weeks. I was shuffling my kids from different relatives while staying with him. Up and down the highway, staying nights at the hospital awaiting him to get enough strength to come home. This was crazy; I never thought I'd be the central character of a TV One movie, yet here I was.

I'm going to leave that craziness there, because my testimony is that I grieved 'my Mama's' death for about 7 to 8 years. Her absence was my faithful companion. I was devoted to it. Her birthdays were super hard; I felt like I couldn't function. Then it was my birthdays; then it was Thanksgiving; then it was Christmas... and OMGee it was the anniversary for her death and her burial. I wouldn't go to church on Mother's Day. I never allowed my kids to celebrate me because I couldn't celebrate 'my Mama.' I was so faithful to that place of darkness... that space of despondency. My life was in limbo because when her life ended, it seemed as if mine did too, to some degree.

Then one day I read a book. Mind you, reading has always been my escape. So, I was reading this book, and in the book, I became really enamored with the central character. Suddenly, it was as if I was slapped upside my head with a mirror, and the image of the main character was me. My spiritual imagination showed me the disgusting reflection of me in all of my misery, narrated through this character, this person, this stranger, yet this familiar spirit. I cried... I cried... I cried. I cried for the little girl, yep, that little girl who kept crying for her mother. I cried for that hollow place that desired the touch of their first known love, the voice of their safety net... the presence of their nurturer.

It was in that space and time that the revelation was so vivid — so dismal — while simultaneously the acknowledgment of *Adonai* was so potent, that I was at a place of repentance, submission and acceptance all at the same time. It was there that the presence of the indwelling Spirit made  itself known to me, and I was ashamed. So ashamed that I had rejected *Adonai*, and even in my innumerable rejections. *He* was still *El Emuwnah*. *He* was faithful to me when I was faithless because *He* is *Adonai*. *His* love never wavered, never changed. No matter what I went through, self-inflicted or victim of circumstance. *He* continued to rescue me. I am so grateful for the blood of *Yeshua* that sealed my destiny, and *He* promised *Abba Father* that *He* wouldn't lose one who belonged to *Elohim*.

My testimony is that I went too far and I stayed too long! I went too far into that dismal, depressed place. I fell into the deception that it's ok to grieve endlessly. That's not of *God*. *He* said to everything there is a season. You see, when I went in, I allowed that devil to close the door and lock it. Every time I would step out, he would trick me back into that place, that forbidden space where I didn't belong. That place was miserable, it was angry, it was hopeless, it was dark and dank, it had a stench, it was mean, it was unrelenting. The deceptive angel of light constantly showed me the realistic picture of depression and injustices of which there was no light.

This book expressed all of these dark emotions that I housed, that I visited, and this book was like that illuminating beam of light... *He* tells us *He* will heal us with *His* beams. Healing transpired upon completion of that read. The insight that I received because I connected with the central character, kindred spirits — I felt like I met the *Father*, the *Son*, and the *Holy Spirit*. I felt like I sat at the table with the *Holy Trinity*, and *they* loved me out of all my iniquity... out of all my faulty perceptions... out of the dark places. I finally found a seat that made me feel like I was seen, that I was heard, that I was felt. Time seemed to have collapsed because I had wasted so much of it. I knew better than going in so far. I knew better than staying so long. Yet I did it. Was it worth it? Truthfully, Abso-Positively-Lutely Yes!

The *Holy Spirit* has awakened a 'knowing' that 'nothing' is wasted. *Abba* uses everything! My scripture during that season was 2 Timothy 1:7, but today as I look in the rearview mirror... it's most definitely Genesis 50:20.

Dr. Nesbitt recently broke down Isaiah 61:4, and she taught on rebuilding the old waste places, a place of restoration. *Adonai* wastes nothing — not your anger, not your rage, not your rebelliousness, not your stony heart, not your betrayals, and not your foolishness. *He* has purpose for your darkest days. It's only when you've been in the fire, like the three Hebrew Boys, that you comprehend that when you come out of the furnace and you don't smell like smoke. That's when you understand that *He* truly knows *His* plans for you... for good and not evil... for prosperity and not insufficiency. It's only when *He* has placed *His* loving hands of healing upon your wretched situations that you can process a portion of grace and mercy that *He* bestows upon you. When you know that you did not deserve *His* unconditional love, but *He* gave it to you anyway! When you receive the revelation that you were one of the ones crucifying *Him* afresh at the Cross on Calvary, and *He* asks for mercy for you. *He* said, "*Father*, forgive <u>**Insert Your Name**</u>, for he/she knows not what he/she does." *Jesus* did that before your entrance on this side of glory because *He* knows all things!

Again, time collapses. That's why I take it seriously when I encounter one who is dealing with loss. All losses are not the same — there are varying situations and degrees. Yet if I meet someone along this last leg of my journey, and I can give them a word of encouragement — trust and believe that the "peace" that *He* has gifted me with — I will indeed share. For whether I live or whether I die, I belong to the *Lord*! I have been giving my testimony of going too far and staying too long for approximately eight years. It means something because there is relevance, and it bears witness of how *He* can indeed take a mess and pour out a message for *His* glory!

I give only *Him* all the glory for it all! I have ascended from peace to peace and have come to walk in "Kingdom Peaces." "Kingdom Peaces" has led me to authentic musings, meanderings, and meditations. It is through my journey of obtaining "Kingdom Peaces", that I pray the *Lord* will illuminate your path to having a better relationship with *Him*. *He* said if *He* be lifted up, *He'd* draw all men. My purpose in penning "Kingdom Peaces" is that *Elohim* will be glorified, that *His* Eternal Word will be edified, and that *His* presence will be revealed to bring healing and deliverance in hidden spaces.

May "Kingdom Peaces" be a place of transparency that you, *His* Beloved, may find solace in your past, present, and your future in the knowledge that *He* is *God* all by *Himself*! *He* knows the "peace" you seek! May they be sown in righteousness in *Jesus Christ*, the righteousness of a fallen world. Our *Rectifier*! Glory be to the *Most High*!

Foreword

Extraordinary! Exceptional! Remarkable! Exclusive! Inclusive! Amazing! Marvelous! Incredible! These are just a few words to describe this unorthodox, and out of the box forward thinking author. Tamela Winfrey's writing style is spiritual, witty, intelligent, transformable, touchable and tangible.

Her ability to captivate you with the *Word of God* will have you gasping for air and screaming for more. This devotional is relative and relatable to all who will read it. This masterpiece is not designed as a pick me-up today and finish next week; it will burst open in you an undeniable hunger and thirst that you didn't know existed.

Tamela is a visionary of *God* who is able to write with pristine accurate sharpness. Her ability to make the *Word* come to life through her writing is nothing less than breathtaking. The title of this masterpiece is "Kingdom Peaces." It is a devotional infused with the *Word of God*. It is uncommon and not like anything that you will ever obtain, in that its purpose is to liberate people of all ages, gender, and race who have been bound by their past, present, and believe it or not, their future because of damaged emotions.

Tamela Winfrey understands that damaged emotions and past trauma are a few of the enemy's vices to keep you from your full potential. This journal will help you to press into the pages of the Word and draw out rivers of living water that will sustain and supply every need to assist you to get to where *God* has preordained you to be. The purpose of "Kingdom Peaces" is authentically designed to give liberation in studying the *Word*, receiving insightful revelations, and instituting a deeper, renewed relationship with *Elohim*, our *Creator*.

As you work on this journal, this journal will start working for you. It will break the hard pillars of your heart and crash through barricades of generational curses and childhood disappointments. "Kingdom Peaces" will birth a purpose in the secret place of your heart and dismantle the secret systems of the kingdom of darkness. Are you ready to live in perfect peace? If so, "Kingdom Peaces" is ready for you!

Renita Hoof
#TheMidwife

THE GREAT PRETENDERS
BY: TAMELA L. WINFREY

Smiling and laughing on the outside
Crying, weeping, sobbing on the inside
Hurt beyond comprehension
Suffering the great losses that can't be recovered on this side

Yet like a thief in the night... a brilliant light appears
The tears cease to flow
The heaviness has lightened
The burdens are yet again bearable

Joy bubbles up in your soul
You walk out of the shadows
You move toward the warmth
You are drawn to that peace

Yes, it's HIM!!!
HE's right there... right there
Where HE's always been
Being all that HE has Always been
HE brought along Grace and Mercy
HE welcomes you in HIS arms and whispers,
"No Charge"
MY love is free and endless
I paid the price for it all
You can leave your baggage at the gate
Only bring a humble spirit that thirsts for the
'living water' that I yearn to give you
Bring in your faith, your trust, and your belief

Yes, I heard when you asked me to help your unbelief
I heard when you prayed for healing
I heard when you prayed for your finances… you wanted to pay your tithes
I heard when you prayed for your family
I heard when you prayed in the still of the night
I heard you at daybreak

I also stored your tears
When sickness came, I stood guard
When death knocked, I decided if you were ready
Remember, I am ELOHIM, the CREATOR
You are MY Masterpiece
I AM the Alpha & the Omega
The AUTHOR & The FINISHER

While you pretend for the world
'The Great Pretenders' are you
Know that I know
I know it all
For I AM the I AM
Ever Present…Omnipotent
All Powerful…Almighty
Know that My Love never expires
I was with you at birth
I will be with you even in death
From 'faith to faith'
From 'strength to strength'
From 'peace to peace'
From 'glory to glory'
From 'everlasting to everlasting'

Signed,
I AM

Table of Contents

Genesis Prayer 1
Alone 4
Ashtray 9
Battles 13
Bitter 17
Borrowed 21
Call It Out 27
Casting 31
Choices 35
Chosen 41
Crossover 47
Edifier 53
El Elyon 57
Esteem 63
Excited 69
Exclusivity 75
Folly 79
Further 85
Good 89
Grateful 95
Greetings 99

Heads And Tails	105
Holy Spirit	109
If	113
Imperfections	117
Keys	123
Knowing	129
Me Me Me	133
Measure	137
Miracles	143
Never	149
Out With the Old	155
Pick	159
Prosper	165
Pusher	169
Rain	175
Reminder	181
Season vs Lifestyle	187
Seekers	193
Servant	199
Trust You	205
Wait	209
Without You	215
Omega Prayer	219
Author's Page	222

Genesis Prayer

Abba Father which art in heaven, hallowed be **Thy Most Holy Name**!

Lord, I bless **Your** Name for **Your** Name is above every name in the heavens, in the earth, and under the earth! Glory be to **You**, O **Most High**! Thank **You Father** for this opportunity to come before **Your** throne of grace once again. Thank **You Lord** for the honor, the privilege to glorify **You Elohim**!

Abba Father, I ask that I decrease that **You** and only **You** increase in this work that **You** authored. I pray that **You** will be glorified with the reading of "Kingdom Peaces", that **Your** distinctive voice is illuminated in the ear of the hearer of **Your** Word. I pray that the execution of **Your** Majesty is magnified within each of these 'peaces' and that there is an unction for worship of **You, Elohim**.

Abba Father, I pray that "Kingdom Peaces" will reap a bountiful harvest for the 'Kingdom of God'; that the remnant **You** speak of will receive the seeds and nurture them. I pray that **Your Word** will bless all that will support this vessel of exhortation.

Abba Father, I pray that "Kingdom Peaces" will be the impetus for someone that feels displaced in life, that the 'peaces' from cover to cover will jump start them with a jolt of joy. I pray that "Kingdom Peaces" will resurrect a melted down spirit, calling forth **Your Word** to remembrance that will empower and renew. I pray that "Kingdom Peaces" will serve as motivation for someone that has lost purpose because of the miscarriages of life as they realize that *You* are still doing a good work in them. I pray that "Kingdom Peaces" will stir up the gift and give courage to someone that has been overlooked and persecuted far too long... that the *'rivers of living water'* will flow like a well-watered spring.

Abba Father, I pray that "Kingdom Peaces" will ignite a newfound relationship between *You* and a son/daughter that got lost on the crooked path of life with even more purpose. I pray that "Kingdom Peaces" will propel someone to meditate intentionally on the 'peaces' and utilize the journal section; that a renewed exuberance will arise as they are led to search *Your Word* diligently and deliberately that *You* might be found.

Abba Father, I ask that *You* and only *You* be glorified. May *You* be exalted in this assignment. May *You* be extolled to the highest degree. May *You* be magnified irrevocably within the pages of "Kingdom Peaces." *Lord God*, I ask that this prayer be **received as a sweet savor before** *Your* 'throne of grace'. May this prayer be sealed by the *Holy Spirit* and washed, cleansed and purified by the *blood of Yeshua*. I present these requests in the 'limitless powerful name' of my *Redeemer*, my *Saviour*, *Jesus*, the *Resurrected Christ*.

Hallelujah Hallelujah Hallelujah!

Amen!

Alone

Joshua 1:5

In this season of weeping and wailing, for there are so many tears shed as we witness the manifestation of the *Word of God* showing *Himself* mighty to the pulling down of strongholds (2 Cor:10:4). We as mere humans are under the construction of the *Greatest Architect*, *Elohim*, and the *Creator* of heaven and earth, who was in the beginning, sometimes find ourselves in a maze. Some of us feel that we are so close to that opening that it will be a portal for release; yet many discern that we, like Joshua are asking the man with the sword at the battle of Jericho, whose side he was on (Josh 5:13). There are instances that you don't know which way to go, who to believe, or who even deserves your loyalty. Lost and alone.

We have loved ones that we worry about... we have loved ones who worry about us. Yet the *Word of God* commands us to: Be anxious for nothing; but in everything by prayer and supplication, with thanksgiving, let your requests be made known unto *God* (Phil 4:6). Let not your heart be troubled: ye believe in *God*, believe also in *Me* (John 14:1).

But how can we not worry, when all we see is death and devastation? Why did my loved one have to die? We needed them for just a little while longer. Why did You take them now, because I don't know how I can do this thing called life without them? Why did *You* take this one; they were good, and *You* left that one who causes trouble and doesn't even regard life as a gift? Why? Why, *Lord*?

Then you have the super-saints' who say, "I don't question the *Lord*", yet in the cloak of darkness, they cry in misery, and their tears murmur the questions that they deny. They laugh and smile and give the correct response; yet in their innermost parts, in the deepest crevice of their soul, they wonder something so simple yet forbidden: 'why?' We're told about Job, our role model for loss; yet, many miss the scriptures where Job questioned the *Lord* (Job 3). How did you miss the *Lamentation of Job?* Job said if he had to suffer, why was he even born (Job 3:11,16)?

Did our *Father* who art in heaven, ever promise that it would be easy? Did *He* promise us no trials... no tribulations... no persecutions... no weeping... no wailing... no tears... no sighing... did *He* ever promise that (Job 14:1)? We all know that the *Word of God* is full of *His* promises, but there are some things that *He* just did not promise. *He* told us in *His inexhaustible Word* that, "In *Me* ye might have peace, and in the world ye shall have tribulation; but... be of good cheer; for *I* have overcome the world (John 16:33)." *He* went further and said, "The sufferings of this present time are not worthy to be compared with the glory which shall be revealed in us (Rom 8:18)." *He* even gave us wisdom for the tears; *He* encourages us, "to count it all joy when we fall into various trials, knowing that the testing of our faith produces patience (James 1:2-3)."

In this season, there are so many who died without loved ones at their bedside, and their loved ones feel that they died alone. Those mourning their death are being tormented with feelings of guilt. We want to always be there, and feel that maybe if we had been there, they would still be here. *His Word* distinctly tells us, "*He* knows the thoughts that *He* thinks toward us, thoughts of peace and not of evil, to give us an expected end (Jer 29:11)."

A person's days are determined; *Elohim* has decreed the number of months and has set limits *He* won't exceed (Job 14:1,5). Whether our loved ones are surrounded by family or fully surrounded by the great cloud of witnesses that reside in the bosom of *Him* that giveth and taketh, they are never alone. *Jehovah Shammah* promised that *He* would never leave nor forsake us (Heb 12:1; Deut 31:8; Heb 13:5).

Despite the intent of the enemy to isolate and separate with that gloom and doom of the nefarious spirit of fear, **Jesus** said that the peace **He** left would be a peace not of this world, and that this world has no authority to take it away... this peace would surpass all understanding because it would have no rhyme or reason, no mathematical equation, no scientific findings... because in the beginning was the **Word** and the **Word** was with **God,** and the **Word** was **God** (John 14:27; John 1:1)!

Come what may, whether it be plagues, diseases, war(s) or rumors of war(s), chaos, or kingdoms of darkness that try to overpower the light; it has no authority, it has no dominion over those who reside under the *shadow of the **Almighty***, nor over those who find their peace in Goshen, nor over those who solely rely on **Jehovah Jirreh** and **El Shaddai** as their source and their supply. For those who trust in **Jehovah Rohi** as the **Lord** being my **Shepherd**, there is an abundance available to them. Through their belief that **He** was, **He** is, and **He** will be; **He** is **Adonai** (My **Lord**) ... **He** is **El Elyon** (the **Lord** of heaven and earth)! You can rest assured that you are never alone! We will never be alone; if we call, trust and believe on the **Name** that is above every name in the heavens, in the earth and beneath the earth (Phil 2:9-10)! The sweetest name I know, **Jesus**!

Musings

What part of this 'Peace' stirred you and why?

_____
_____
_____
_____
_____
_____

Meanderings

Did this 'Peace' trigger any particular memory and why?

_____
_____
_____
_____
_____
_____
_____

Meditations

What secret place will you allow **Jehovah Rapha** to minister to you as you ponder this 'Peace'?

Ashtray

Colossians 1:16-17

The ashtray is heavy duty. It's sturdy. It's deep. It may be cracked, but it holds true to form and performs what it was created to do. It's always there. It's usually not the most attractive, but it is dependable. And more often than not, it's full. It stays full because it is steadfast; people use it and forget about it. It's an afterthought. Now that people no longer smoke inside, it's left outside. It withstands the downpouring of rain, the fall of snow, and ice; the heat of the dog days of summer. Sometimes it smells, and people speak of its' need to be emptied, but not many try to fulfill the need. It's only seen as a dumping place.

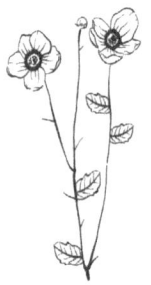

That's a position that some people will allow themselves to play. They are the wind beneath the wings. They are the sounding boards. They are the wisdom that you can't find in a book; they always have a word of encouragement. But once people have dumped all of their ashes and moved along on their journey, the ashtray is remembered no more (Gal 6:2). Despite all that the ashtray has taken in, receiving someone else's ashes, being of enormous service to others, the ashtray only accessorizes the wall as decoration — still full of other people's ashes.

Have you ever stopped to consider your ashtray? When you get so full of life, you go to that person and maybe you never say what's truly in your heart. But there is something about just hearing their voice and your freedom to chit-chat for a bit. Once you leave that person's presence, life feels lighter. What once seemed so heavy has dissipated into... ashes. Wow! The chain has been broken; the weight lost its density; the faulty mission was aborted. Why? Because that ashtray is solid, its' depth is undefined. It may be cracked; you might not openly acknowledge the wisdom that the ashtray delivers, but its revelation holds its form and gives you what you didn't even know you needed.

God said *He* would use the foolishness of the world to confound the wise. Never discount the marred... the disfigured... the misused. Never disregard the forgotten. Never discard what man calls useless. *God* said that *He* uses all things. All things were created by *Him*, for *Him*, and by *Him* all things consist. Visible and invisible, thrones, dominions, principalities, powers — whatever it may be, it was all created by *Him*. Even the ashtrays have a purpose (Col 1:16-17).

Musings

What part of this 'Peace' stirred you and why?

_____
_____
_____
_____
_____
_____

Meanderings

Did this 'Peace' trigger any particular memory and why?

_____
_____
_____
_____
_____
_____

Meditations

What secret place will you allow **Jehovah Rapha** to minister to you as you ponder this 'Peace'?

Battles

2 Chronicles 20:15

There is a battle that always seems to await you from the moment you open your eyes and give **God** the glory for a new day's mercy as well as the time you prepare your daily regimen. There's a trap that is laid out for you; a snare that beckons you each and every day.

In life, we find ourselves constantly fighting. Fighting to live and fighting to love; fighting to survive, fighting to overcome, fighting to hold our peace; fighting to keep our person, fighting to keep our sanity, and finally fighting for our promises. And in the midst of the fight, we ask **God**, why so many battles? Why must we fight so much and so hard?

A person once asked me why there were so many battles in the Old Testament of the Bible and none in the New Testament. That question plagued me for quite a while. And the *Holy Spirit* told me that the greatest battles we face are within (Eph 6:12). ***Jesus Christ*** won it all when **He** got on the Cross on Calvary. **He** gave **His** life that we might have life and have it in abundance (John 10:10).

This is something many know. To a certain degree we understand, but we still find ourselves in warfare. Have you ever noticed that sometimes when a person is on their deathbed, they seem to linger? They have separated from this side, but there is still that one thread that holds on past man's prediction.

I truly feel that we have fought so many

battles to live that we don't know how to stop fighting... even when it's our desire to go home to *Father*. Human nature still wants to toil and stay with loved ones on this side. We sing and speak of going home to worship *Him* all day long, but the heart of man wrestles with the separation from this side of glory. The warfare is but a distraction to keep you from totally leaning and depending on our *Savior* (Prov 3:5).

We have to renew our minds daily by meditating on the *everlasting Word*, (Rom 12:2). When we allow the *Word of God* to saturate our entire being, we will learn to relax in *God*. We will discover that the hills and mountains have already been leveled. That crooked road that zig-zagged for miles and miles has been straightened. The valley that was sung so low is filled with praise, and you can praise your way right on out! And good *Lord*, that rough patch that haunted you every time you closed your eyes is smoother than silk sheets (Isa 40:3-4). The battle never belonged to you (2 Chr 20:15).

Father was just waiting on you to recognize that *He* is mighty in battle (Psa 24:8). Not only is *He* mighty in battle; *He is Jehovah Gibbor*, the *Lord God* mighty in battle. *His* arm has not grown short, nor will it ever (Num 11:23). *He* is *Omnipotent! He* is all powerful! Almighty! Everlasting! Eternal! *He* never lost a battle!

Musings

What part of this 'Peace' stirred you and why?

_____
_____
_____
_____
_____
_____

Meanderings

Did this 'Peace' trigger any particular memory and why?

_____
_____
_____
_____
_____
_____
_____

Meditations

What secret place will you allow **Jehovah Rapha** to minister to you as you ponder this 'Peace'?

Bitter
Exodus 15:22-27

Bitterness reeks of disdain, nastiness, dissatisfaction and gravitates to anger, hate, and evil. Life happens to the very best of us, and sometimes it tackles the best that is in us. It may blindside you with an Iron Mike Tyson punch, or it may charm you with the subtlety of Muhammad Ali with fancy footwork, rhythmic jive talk, and a pretty face... but the dregs are less than pleasing.

Many times, you may find yourself stealing away to a safe place and backtracking on this journey you've tread how many millions of times to try to arrive with a different answer, but every time, it's always the same response. No matter how charismatic you are, no matter how intelligent you may be, sometimes you cannot re-write the story... the **Author** and **Finisher** of your faith has allowed the orchestration of the narrative. **He** knows the ending just as well as the beginning... **He** is **Alpha** and **Omega** (Rev 22:13)!

There are bitter pills that have to be swallowed. There are deep waters to be tread. There are wildfires that have to be extinguished. There are waters that have pieces of wood thrown into them to make what once was bitter... sweet. **Elohim** is so loving that **He** makes bitter experiences sweet (Exod 15:22-27).

It's only after you've mastered the storm that you have the ability to witness yourself walking on water for the *glory of **God***. Only a loving ***God*** would give us the structure as well as the liberty to live an abundant life. Only after you've come out of the storm do you find honor in the rainbow and its true significance (Gen 9:11-16).

The aftermath is poignant because many situations we go through are self-inflicted… but our ***Justifier*** assures us that many are the afflictions of the righteous; but ***He*** delivers us out of them all (Psa 34:19). ***God*** will never allow us to go through tribulations or temptations that we are not equipped to overcome without preparing an escape for us (1 Cor 10:13). ***He*** loves us so much; ***He*** knows that ***His*** children will encounter some harsh circumstances, but ***He*** knows the thoughts ***He*** thinks toward us. And ***He*** moves as ***He*** moves, blessing and cursing whom ***He*** will (Jer 29:11). The bittersweet may not be understood, but it's in the misunderstanding that we receive revelation and understanding that ***I Am*** has all power and might in ***His*** righteous right hand, and ***He*** knows your beginning, which some call your ending (Psa 147:5). Being in ***Christ*** is always the beginning — in the beginning was the *Word*. Take it and eat it up; and it shall make thy belly bitter; but it shall be in thy mouth sweet as honey (Rev 10:9).

Musings

What part of this 'Peace' stirred you and why?

_____
_____
_____
_____
_____
_____
_____

Meanderings

Did this 'Peace' trigger any particular memory and why?

_____
_____
_____
_____
_____
_____
_____

Meditations

What secret place will you allow **Jehovah Rapha** to minister to you as you ponder this 'Peace'?

Borrowed

Romans 14:8

Something old, something new, something borrowed, something blue — sound familiar? Sounds like wedding bells to me. Something that makes you happy... perhaps something to make you smile.

Not everyone is excited about the process of borrowing. Yet we wake up every day to another day's journey that's borrowed. It's a loan because it has to be returned to the sender. We praise **God** for health and strength that is borrowed because **He** is the *Author* and *Finisher* of our faith (Heb 12:2). We are ever so grateful for the use of these borrowed tombs, these shells that house our most precious gift from **God**—the *indwelling* **Holy Spirit** (1 Cor 6:19).

Jesus was birthed into this world by immaculate conception in a place not fit for the *King* of kings. ***Jesus*** was buried after **His** crucifixion in a borrowed tomb... a wealthy man stepped out of his comfortable place and professed his belief in the **Messiah** (Matt 27:57-60). The *Word* tells us that the wealth of the wicked is laid up for the just (Ecc 2:26). Some who focus on the borrowed tomb should center on the purpose of it being borrowed. ***Jesus*** knew **He** would give it back in 3 days—it was only a loan for a little while (Luke 24:1-7).

When the **Messiah** stood in the midst of **His** adversaries, **He** never cowered. **He** never backed down from sound doctrine. **He** spoke with authority and dominion, for **He** stood as the *Author* (John 1:1) as **He** taught the intentional interpretation of the scriptures (Matt 22:15-46). **He** suited up the apostles for the perilous times ahead, times of persecution, the season during which many of them would become martyrs for **His** name's sake (John 15:18-25). ***Jesus*** said, 'Fear them not that can kill the body, but are not able to kill the soul' (Matt 10:28).

Why? Because our corruptible body must return to the dust from whence it came. Remember, it's only loaned to us for a small measure of time (Ecc 3:20).

When we stand at the grave of a loved one who has finished their race and we cry, we must know that weeping only endures for the night because joy comes in the morning (Psa 30:5). For our loved ones who left us in **Christ** stepped into **God's** great glory and were greeted with that promised joy in the morning. To everything there is a season, and a time to every purpose under the heaven: A time to be born and a time to die. There's a time to return the borrowed tomb; it has served its purpose, and **God** has retrieved the spirit that was loaned to the earth (Ecc 3:1-2).

Our loved ones aren't ours; they are vessels that **God** placed in our lives, but it was only an assignment. They had purpose in our lives — fathers to aid in the planting of the seed, mothers in the nurturing of the seed, parents in the training up of the seed to be for the glory of our **Heavenly Father**. All serve their purpose for their appointed time to walk in authority over the task that **Father** ordained for each of us—from the least to the greatest.

And as we draw nearer to **Elohim**, **He** is so gracious to disclose purpose in us as **He** orders our footsteps (James 4:8). We are to give thanks at all times and remember all **His** benefits; for they are as innumerable as the angels in heaven (Psa 103:2). We should be grateful for our parents, our siblings, our spouses, our children, our extended family, for we are rejoicing together in the season of reunions on this earth.

If you close your natural eyes, open your spiritual eyes. Wherefore, seeing we also are compassed about with so great a cloud of witnesses, let us lay aside every weight (Heb 12:1). Envision the reunion of the spirits who leave their borrowed tombs that had begun to decay and betray. Our bodies don't have the same vigor at 40 that they had at 20, and that's a whole lot of grace, because many don't even see 50 years of age. At 70, the ignoring of pain isn't as tolerable as it was in your 40s.

With each new year, we should come into a renewed divine revelation that grace has kept us and mercy has covered us, and that **Adonai** knows all things! That's why **He** wants us to put all of our trust in **Him** and understand that this life we live is fleeting — temporary — and all that we amass will decay, and we will leave it behind (2 Cor 4:18). All the treasures we attain — spouses, children, siblings, parents, the mansions, the expensive cars, the dazzling jewelry, the designer duds — we will leave all this stuff behind, because **He** gave it to us as temporary. It won't hold its value.

What is it to gain the whole world and lose your soul (Mark 8:36)? We have to invest in the eternal, because we seek to serve an **Eternal God**, an **Everlasting God** that loves us so much, **He** ordains borrowed time for you (James 4:14). Make the most of your borrowed time. Count it all joy, your borrowed time. Don't lose yourself trying to build up something that doesn't belong to you, for **God** will redeem all that is **His**. Build your hope on things that are eternal. Build up your spirit that is everlasting in the love of **God**, for nothing, and no one can separate you from **His** eternal love (Rom 8:38-39)! Choose today: borrowed or eternal.

Musings

What part of this 'Peace' stirred you and why?

_____
_____
_____
_____
_____
_____

Meanderings

Did this 'Peace' trigger any particular memory and why?

_____
_____
_____
_____
_____
_____

Meditations

What secret place will you allow **Jehovah Rapha** to minister to you as you ponder this 'Peace'?

Call It Out

Romans 3:23

Call it out! Call it out! Whatever is sabotaging your destiny, call that devil out! Call it what it is, and once you call it out, tell it, 'The **Lord** rebuke thee' (Zech 3:2). When you call it out, it loses its momentum and it loses power.

Sin will cripple you because it becomes too heavy. You find yourself searching for 'you.' Sin will steal your identity to where you no longer have a name; your sin becomes your name. Your sin is what people speak of; they will say, 'You know, the one who steals all the time; you can't leave them in the room by themselves,' or 'You know, the one who lies all the time' or 'the one who cheated on her husband' or 'the one who cusses her mother out.' Your sin will signify your very being.

The good thing in all of this is that you don't have to wear your sin all the days of your life. Sin was conquered by our **Lord** and **Savior, Jesus Christ**. **He** came that we wouldn't have to live in our sin without an escape. **He** shed **His** blood that there might be remission of sin (Matt 26:28).

God sent **His** only begotten **Son** into the world that we might live in **Him** (John 3:16). **Jesus** was the propitiation for our sins, the *ultimate sacrifice*—one that you and I aren't qualified for (1 John 2:2). **Jesus Christ** committed no sin; neither was deceit in **His** mouth (1 Pet 2:22). **He** was blameless, without a spot or a wrinkle. As much effort as we place in trying to live holy, there's always a

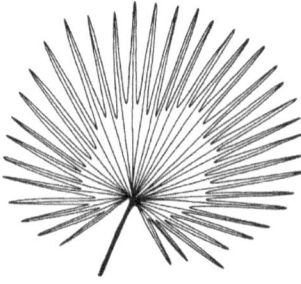

snare; some are so small, you almost miss the fact that it is still sin.

Jesus was so loving and kind that *He* made *Himself* worthy of no reputation. *He* didn't come in *His* heavenly glory; but took upon the flesh of a servant, and humbled *Himself* unto death, even the death of the cross (Phil 2:6). *He* loves us implicitly; *He* loves us beyond reciprocity. And when *He* conquered death, *He* was resurrected and ascended into heaven. *He* said, "No Charge."

The story didn't end there. *He* sits at the right hand of the *Father* and makes intercession on our behalf daily (Heb 7:25). Understand that the price of sin is too great to continue to invest in it; call it out. If we confess our sins, *El Emuwnah* is faithful to forgive our sins and to cleanse us from all unrighteousness (1 John 1:9). Refuse to be held hostage by your sins. Allow them to rest in the past by calling them out and pleading the *blood of Jesus* for the remission of your sins. *He* is well able!

Musings

What part of this 'Peace' stirred you and why?

_____
_____
_____
_____
_____
_____
_____

Meanderings

Did this 'Peace' trigger any particular memory and why?

_____
_____
_____
_____
_____
_____
_____

Meditations

What secret place will you allow **Jehovah Rapha** to minister to you as you ponder this 'Peace'?

Casting

1 Peter 5:7

When I think of the word 'casting', I instantly see a spindly fisherman casting his line into the water expecting a spectacular catch as he trains his young apprentice the art and the love of fishing. But upon further retrospection, my mind is triggered to the art of life, love, and its irrevocable lessons.

In life, we will encounter situations that grieve us and frustrate us, and most people are urged to confront the issue. Confront your Goliath with immeasurable wisdom and strength, and prepare to see *Jehovah Nissi* come in and do only what *He* can do — lift you up with *His* 'banner of love' (Song 2:4). What happens when you're only met with a brick wall and you're even more disturbed, so frustrated that it has now honed into the energy of anger?

Not all battles are to be confronted; some are to be inspected and released. How so? Humble yourselves, therefore, under the mighty hand of *God*, that *He* may exalt you in due time, casting all your care upon *Him*, for *He* cares for you (James 4:10; 1 Pet 5:7). If it concerns you, it concerns *Him*. *He* knows the adversary's strategies far better than anyone; the adversary has to come to *Father* before he can approach you… because *God* cares for you (Zech 3:1).

Guess what? *God* gives us strict instructions. *He* said, 'Be not afraid nor dismayed by reason of this great multitude (of trials and tribulations); for the battle is not yours, but *God's*' (2 Chr 20:15). That which you cast upon troubled waters to *Him*, *He's* already fixed it. *He* did that! Why? Because when we are faithless, *He* remains faithful;

He cannot deny *Himself*. *He* cannot disown us who are a part of *Himself*, and *He* will always carry out *His* promises (2 Tim 2:13). *He* is *El Emuwnah*! If it concerns you, it concerns *Him*! *He* is attentive to *His* own!

Mother E has sown a seed of wisdom in me as I sit under her tutelage. She always tells me, cast thy bread upon the water, for thou shalt find it after many days (Ecc 11:1). The seed of good works—good will—shall multiply when given with an open hand. Give, and it shall be given unto you; good measure, pressed down, shaken together, and running over, shall men give into your bosom. For with the same measure that you use it shall be measured to you again (Luke 6:38). There will be a return in *Jesus*' *Name*! Cast works for the good when *Jesus* is at the beginning, in the middle, and always at the end (*Adonai*) for *He* will never leave you nor forsake you, *Jehovah Shammah* (Heb 13:8).

Trust in the *Lord* with all thine heart; and lean not to thine own

understanding. In all thy ways acknowledge *Him*, and *He* shall direct thy path, (Prov 3:5,6) *He* is *El Emuwnah*!! You can trust *Him* when you are unable to trace *Him*! *He* is magnificent! *He* is majesty!! *He* is honored! *He* is undefined! *He* is so sovereign that *He* has to swear by *Himself*, because there is nothing and no one greater than *Him* (Heb 6:13). *He* is *Elohim*, *God* all by *Himself*, the great *Creator*!

Musings

What part of this 'Peace' stirred you and why?

_____
_____
_____
_____
_____
_____
_____

Meanderings

Did this 'Peace' trigger any particular memory and why?

_____
_____
_____
_____
_____
_____
_____

Meditations

What secret place will you allow **Jehovah Rapha** to minister to you as you ponder this 'Peace'?

Choices

Joshua 24:15

Choose ye this day whom ye will serve (Josh 24:15). On this journey, you will encounter many spaces in time. You will come to a juncture where you will be confronted with situations that introduce a stage that calls for choices. The decisions that will await you aren't always pleasant, nor are they always easy; but they definitely are necessary. Life would be simpler if we could just meander through without trials, tribulations, and fanfare, but what would life be without choices?

Moses told the Israelites about choices consistently. There was a choice between life and death: a blessing or a curse. Moses encouraged them to choose life. We also must pattern ourselves after this example in choosing life, not just for ourselves but also for our descendants (Deut 30:19).

Trials and tribulations come to strengthen you, because it's in the battle that you discover the warrior within. Will you shrink back because of your visualization? Do you envision giants or grasshoppers? Can you envision victory over defeat? What do your eyes behold? Life and death are in the power of the tongue, and those who love it shall eat the fruit thereof. For by your words, you will be justified, and by your words you will be condemned (Num 13:33; Prov 18:21; Matt 12:37).

I've always heard, *'Never bring a knife to a gunfight.'* And I've been told,

'Don't pull out a gun unless you're ready to shoot.' In battle, we have to make choices. We have to choose our weapon of warfare. Paul instructs us in the 6th chapter of Ephesians how to suit up and boot up for battle, instructing the warrior to put on the full armor of **God**. After naming the weapons of warfare, Paul breaks it down to the simplest element of any battle. Pray in the *Spirit* on all occasions with all kinds of prayers and requests (Eph 6:13-18). The most victorious battles are won in worship. Believers know beyond a shadow of a doubt that every knee will bow and every tongue will confess **Jesus** as **Lord** (Phil 2:10).

Jesus is our weapon of choice. **He** is called the **Lion of Judah** and the **Lamb of God** (John 1:36)! The great prophet John discloses that in his translation by a divine vision, one of the elders told him to weep not, for the **Lion of Judah**, the **Root of David**, has triumphed (Rev 5:5)! **He** was the only one able to open the scroll to stop the destruction of mankind; everything that needed to be done to  secure our right to live eternally was satisfied by the **Lamb of God**. **He** died an unjustified sinner's death, but rose as the **Resurrected Christ**, victorious over all the wiles of the devil — even the yoke of bondage deemed death! **He** overcame it all!

Every step **He** took, **He** took that we might have the right to choose eternal life in **Him**. **He** endured many injustices in order to comprehend our infirmities and sufferings throughout time, even in 2021. When **He** intercedes on our behalf, **He** understands what we are experiencing. **He's** been there. **He's** done that (Isa 53:4). Not because **He** deserved it, but because **He** chose to — **He** chose you! **He** chose me! **He** chose us before the worlds was formed (Eph 1:4)! **He** loves us even knowing we aren't worthy of all **He** has done in our stead. **He** took our sins, that we might become the righteousness of **God** in **Him** who knew no sin! **Jesus**, the **Angel of the Lord** (2 Cor 5:21)!

Pray in faith to the one who can extinguish the fiery darts of the enemy! Pray when you feel the persecution of your enemies on every side! Pray when you're wounded by the merciless attacks on you by your family, those closest to you! Pray when you don't feel as if it will make a difference. Acknowledge that the enemy will tell you your prayers will fall to the ground; but we know that he is the father of lies (John 8:44). Pray when you don't know what to pray for (Rom 8:26). Bow before your **Master**, and call upon the *Name* that is above every name in the heavens, in the earth, and under the earth!

Pray because prayer changes things! Pray like Enoch... Pray like Elijah... Pray like Daniel in the lion's den... Pray like Shadrach, Meshach and Abednego... Pray like Jehoshaphat... Pray like Gideon... Pray like Esther... Pray like Stephen... Pray like ***Jesus*** (1 Thes 5:16-18)!

Choose eternal life today! Choose ***Jesus Christ*** as your **Savior**! Choose ***Jesus Christ*** as your deliverer! Choose ***Jesus Christ*** as your weapon of choice! ***Jesus Christ*** is the fulfillment of the Old Testament... *His* grace is sufficient (2 Cor 12:9)!

In all of that, there really isn't much of a choice if you are a child of the **Most High**. Choose **Christ**, not just because you fell in love with *Him*, but because *He* first loved you (1 John 4:19)! Choose ye whom ye shall serve this day; for there is *One God* (Josh 24:15)! ***Elohim***, the ***Creator*** of the heavens and earth and the fullness thereof!

#KINGDOMPEACES

Musings

What part of this 'Peace' stirred you and why?

_____
_____
_____
_____
_____
_____

Meanderings

Did this 'Peace' trigger any particular memory and why?

_____
_____
_____
_____
_____
_____
_____

Meditations

What secret place will you allow **Jehovah Rapha** to minister to you as you ponder this 'Peace'?

_____
_____
_____
_____
_____
_____
_____
_____
_____
_____
_____
_____
_____
_____
_____

Chosen

Acts 10:34

Chosen is a phrase that makes one feel special. Chosen insinuates that one is picked out from the crowd. More often than not, that individual walks in that anointing, always called forth from the crowd. It can be a good thing, to some, even a wonderful thing. But it may rob one of understanding the less fortunate. The one who may sit faithfully in the pew. One who is diligent in praying for e-ve-ry-bo-dy!!! If you have never sat on the outside looking in, you will never understand the viewpoint of the observer — one who wishes to be seen, to be heard, to be acknowledged. Picked out to be honored is an honor to the honoree.

So, what is it about those who never seem to make the cut? Their accomplishments seem to be valued at nil and appear to be null and void. Is it a wonder why some people are never able to grasp the bruised emotions that the overlooked, unappreciated and forgotten tuck away? Is there anyone who understands? There is one that tells us that when man forgets, *God* remembers.

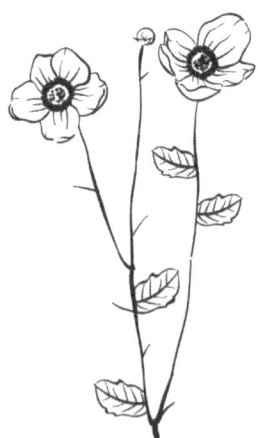

The *Father* tells us that the first shall be last and the last shall be first (Matt 20:16). *He* said that *He* wouldn't forget us; that we would be inscribed in *His* hand (Isa 49:16). Many times, one may get discouraged because of the reception of negativity that you are not good enough; that you never measure up; that

 you will never have what it takes to reach your desired stature. **Father God** told us to be not conformed to this world, but to be transformed by the renewing of our minds in **Christ** (Rom 12:2). In **Jesus Christ**, there is one body, one spirit (Eph 4:4). Guess what? In **Christ**, there are no big 'I's, or little 'you's', for our **Father** is no respecter of persons (Acts 10:34). **His** love is unconditional. **He** bears no preference of one over another; **His** love as **El Elyon** is unchanging and everlasting. **He** wants the best for **His** children, even when we are in disobedience. Whom the **Father** seals with **His Word** never has to feel inadequate or worthless, because **God** gave **His** only begotten **Son** that whosoever believed would not perish, but would have everlasting life (John 3:16).

There is an abundance with your name. There is an overflow with your name. There is grace with your name on it. There is no lack or insufficiency in your reward because you are chosen to be **His** child who lives for **Christ**.

Stop wasting precious time waiting for people to recognize you or choose you when in actuality, what they say or do matters not. Only what **Elohim** declares and decrees over you lasts. **His** Words... **His** works... **His** desires for you anoints you with destiny in **Jesus Christ**. In essence, when you begin to sow into that voice of negativity, instead seek solace and affirmation in the **Word of God** that assures you that you are fearfully and wonderfully made (Psa 139:14).

Offer sacrifices of joy as **He** lifts up thine head above others (Psa 3:3). Put not your trust in status and position, because that power belongs to **God**; for **God** renders to every man according to **His** work (Job 34:11). A seeker of **God** and **His** righteousness doesn't have to allow the fickleness of society to determine or obliterate what **God** has already ordained; **He** seals **His** chosen.

Many are called, but few are chosen... **God's** strategy will astonish as

His chosen may not coincide with man's definition of chosen. For *God* takes the foolishness of the world to confound the wise (Matt 22:14; 1 Cor 1:27). Walk in your *God*-given direction, for in that journey there is joy. Stand before the *Father* as *His* 'Chosen' vessel, willing and able to be *His* obedient servant — not called but chosen. Remember, you are a chosen people, a royal priesthood, a holy nation, *GOD's* special possession, that you may declare the praises of *Him*, who called you out of darkness into *His* wonderful light (1 Pet 2:9).

#KINGDOMPEACES

Musings

What part of this 'Peace' stirred you and why?

_____
_____
_____
_____
_____
_____

Meanderings

Did this 'Peace' trigger any particular memory and why?

_____
_____
_____
_____
_____
_____

Meditations

What secret place will you allow **Jehovah Rapha** to minister to you as you ponder this 'Peace'?

_____
_____
_____
_____
_____
_____
_____
_____
_____
_____
_____
_____
_____
_____
_____
_____
_____

Crossover

Psalm 32:8

Side to side. Passing by. You let me by. I'll let you by. The Crossover. The Crossover is indicative of movement seeking a particular destination. There is a desire to go from point A to point B, and there awaits a prize at the desired destination.

The Crossover may be a lifetime journey or it may be seasonal. It's a pivotal moment in one's life where there has to be movement. There is a spiritual mandate on your life. Sometimes we find ourselves stagnant in a space that is not conducive to our growth or our hopes and dreams. This complacency is a bit too comfortable, and that's your first inkling that it's time to move. In our lifetime, we should always be seeking more. *Christ* came that we might have more abundant life — not a small portion, not a couple of slices of mediocrity, but that we might have it more abundantly (John 10:10). *He* instructs us to live each day like it's our last, because no man knows the day nor the hour (Matt 24:36-51).

When we see a rainbow, we should rejoice at that token that *He* intentionally placed in the sky to remind us that *Elohim* is a *Promise-Keeper*. That secret hope you've housed for 25 years, tucked into your closet full of forgotten dreams — now, after all of these years of being hidden, the *Holy Spirit* reawakens that dream, bringing it to the forefront and placing it in your direct vision (John 14:26; Joel 2:28). But because of the timespan, your confidence has dwindled as you rationalize the many reasons that say, 'impossible.' 'It's too late.' 'I'm too old.' 'I can't.' 'It's for someone else.' 'My season has passed.' Gift-wrapped untruths from the father of lies (John 8:44).

You're at a pivotal moment in time. A time that requires action. You have to choose this day whom you will serve (Josh 24:15). Do you serve the *God* who says 'All things are possible through *Christ*' (Phil 4:13)? Or do you serve the god of fear and denial? *Elohim* said *He* would renew your youth like the eagles, and *He* can redeem the time (Psa 103:5). *He* commands time... and time obeys. *He's* the gleam of light that shines its beam through your window pane and radiates iridescent light on your kitchen counter. *He's* the reflection of the rainbow on the signs that you zoom past on the highway. *El Chayil*, is the bank that stored your memory for such a time as this, that you can recall this deep seeded desire. *He* will allow you to sit back and 'watch the show' because *He* is the *Movie Producer*! *He* is the *Director* who yells, "Cut!" *He* is also the *Speaker of the House* who calls forth those things that be not as though they were... because *He* can!

But you have to make up your mind to get up and cross over to the other side. The Israelites had 'many waters to cross.' They went into enemy territory. They went into foreign lands. And with each new venture, they had to bow down and be obedient as they crossed over.

God continually showed *Himself* mighty. They witnessed *Jehovah Nissi* as *God* raised up a standard over them — *His* unconditional love, their banner of victory. They were called to a higher purpose.

In order to cross over, you have to go through some things. There will be some delays as *He's* teaching you that the delay isn't a denial. You are in a holding pattern. Patience has its own perfect work (James 1:4). *He* had some seeds that had to be sown into you that would build you so that you could handle the task at hand.

When we are young, we are fearless, and sometimes our fearless nature can be our downfall. But **God** knows all, so there is a need for a crossover, but there is also a lesson that precedes the blessing. Our **Father** doesn't always bless us according to our wants and desires, just as **He** doesn't give us what our sins deserve. **He** knows the times and seasons of our lives (Psa 103:10). **He** knows our time span. **He** knows the number of hairs on our heads. **He** knows when we are ready for a crossover (Luke 12:7).

He knows. We have to trust in **His** knowing because **He** is the everlasting compass in our lives. **He** is not like man-made compasses that will sometimes go awry or break. **He** is indestructible! So, as we allow **Him** to not only encompass us with designated angels, we have to allow **Him** to be the compass that will lead, guide, and direct us. We have to know that **His** thoughts and ways are far above ours (Isa 55:8).

That's why we are attempting to cross over, because in the crossover, there are better days ahead. When we are blessed to cross over to **Christ,** there is a just reward for the rest of our lives. We must hear **Him** say, "Arise, shine; for thy light is come, and the glory of the **Lord** is risen upon thee" (Isa 60:1).

Favor has prospered your path, and it's time to cross over to the greater that awaits you. The crossover may be your salvation when you truly accept **Jesus** as the **Resurrected Christ** as your **Lord and Savior**, as the **Redeemer** of your soul. Your crossover may be when you walk in your purpose allowing the anointing to flow uninhibited, for out of your belly shall flow rivers of living water (John 7:38). Your crossover may be when you enter *Eternal Life*, for this place is not our home; we are foreigners passing through (1 Chr 29:15).

Whatever your crossover may be, may it always be in **Christ**, with **Christ**, and for **Christ**. Just walk in obedience and cross over.

Musings

What part of this 'Peace' stirred you and why?

_____
_____
_____
_____
_____
_____

Meanderings

Did this 'Peace' trigger any particular memory and why?

_____
_____
_____
_____
_____
_____
_____

Meditations

What secret place will you allow **Jehovah Rapha** to minister to you as you ponder this 'Peace'?

_____
_____
_____
_____
_____
_____
_____
_____
_____
_____
_____
_____
_____
_____
_____

Edifier

1 Thessalonians 5:11

May you be edified this day by the *Edifier*!

May you be enriched in your spirit this day by the *Edifier*! (1 Cor 1:5)

May you be enlightened this day by the *Edifier*! (Eph 1:18)

May your latter be enlarged this day by the *Edifier*! (Job 8:7)

May you be positioned under an open heaven this day by the *Edifier*! (Deut 28:12)

May your broken heart be mended this day by the *Edifier*! (Psa 147:3)

May your strength be strengthened this day by the *Edifier*! (Psa 84:7)

May your faith be heightened this day by the *Edifier*! (Luke 17:5)

May your knowledge of the *Word of God* be stretched this day by the *Edifier*! (2 Tim 2:15)

May your soul and your mind be renewed with the purifying blood of the *Edifier*! (Phil 4:8)

May your worship be pleasing to the *Edifier*! (1 Chr 16:29)

May you always be encouraged by the *Edifier*! (Josh 1:9)

May you grow in relationship with the *Edifier*! (Zech 1:3)

May your hearing be cognizant to the voice of the *Edifier*! (John 10:27)

May your eye be revelatory to the works of the *Edifier*! (Exod 14:13)

May your feet dance to the beat of the heart of the *Edifier*! (Psa 149:3)

May your hands war for the glory of the *Edifier*! (Psa 144:1)

May your scent emit the sweetest fragrance to the *Edifier*! (Eze 20:41)

May you comfort fellow believers each day that **God** gives you breath in the exaltation of the *Edifier*! (1 Thes 5:11)

May the first fruits of your lips exalt the *Edifier*! (Heb 13:15)

May your birth and death be a testament of the power of the *Edifier*! (Rom 14:8)

May the reader of the psalm give glory to the **Most High** and exalt the *Edifier*! (Rev 1:3)

But seek ye first the *kingdom of God*, and **His** righteousness; and all these things shall be added unto you. (Matt 6:33)

May the believer in the **Resurrected Christ** find joy in their mission to *edify* someone along this journey.

Musings

What part of this 'Peace' stirred you and why?

_____
_____
_____
_____
_____
_____

Meanderings

Did this 'Peace' trigger any particular memory and why?

_____
_____
_____
_____
_____
_____

Meditations

What secret place will you allow **Jehovah Rapha** to minister to you as you ponder this 'Peace'?

El Elyon

1 Chronicles 29:11

The *Lord* is my shepherd; I shall not want (Psa 23:1).

Jehovah Rohi assures me that I shall not want for any good or beneficial thing, for *Jehovah Jireh* has already provided all my needs according to *His* glorious riches that never cease to flow (Psa 34:10).

Elohim, our *Creator* is so good! *He* constantly reminds us that old things have passed away; behold all things have become new. We rest under that with each new day when *He* calls us forth into new graces and unimaginable mercies that leave us in awe of just how great is our *God* (Isa 65:17).

El Shaddai, our *God* of blessings, seeks to bless us as we are led to bless others for the glory of the *Most High* (Acts 20:35)!

When we begin to shun the world of confusion and pursue peace with passion, our walk and our talk changes in the place where we are overshadowed by *Jehovah Shalom* with the unusual peace that surpasses all understanding as it blankets our mind in *Christ Jesus* (Phil 2:5).

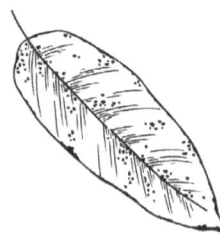

We find ourselves separated from others, from our normal, as *Jehovah M'Kaddesh* sifts us for a greater purpose in *Elohim* (2 Thes 2:13).

During the sanctification season, we encounter *El Emuwnah*, our faithful *God*, *He* who remains faithful when we find ourselves faithless. There is a purification process in sanctification, and our old mindset may seek a comfortable seat of complacency; an atmosphere that seems kinder and safer, not understanding that *His* word really will not return unto *Him* void. We must complete the test.

You have to go through the fire so that you can run back and tell that you didn't get burned, nor did you even come out smelling like smoke, for how great is our ***God, Jehovah Gibbor***, the ***Lord God***, mighty in battle. *He* promised that *He* wouldn't lose one of *His* own (Psa 24:8).

Jehovah Shammah beckons us to rest under the shadow of the ***Almighty***, to be refreshed and revived in the knowledge that ***Abba Father*** is a *promise-keeper* (Psa 91:1). *He* will never leave us nor forsake us.

In our period of sin-sickness, ***Jehovah Tsidkenu*** became sin, that we might become the righteousness of the living and true ***God*** in our covering, ***Jesus Christ*** (2 Cor 5:21).

When death crept in, unbeknownst to you, surprising you in the midst of consecration, you called upon ***Jehovah Rapha***. Didn't *He* make those bitter experiences as sweet as a kiss to a newborn babe, because *He* breathed a resurrected life into you as *He* rebuked the destroyer? And you can testify as an over-comer that you lived through a *Modern Day Passover* in 2020-2022. Covid-19 had to pass over; we acknowledge that the weapon did indeed form, but glory be to ***Jehovah Nissi***; it did not prosper. In ***Jehovah Shammah***, we can take comfort as the ***Holy Spirit***, our ***Comforter***, will not leave us ignorant to the wiles of the enemy of our soul (Isa 54:17).

Jehovah did not give us the spirit of fear, but of love, of power, and of a sound mind. Even if you find yourself on your sickbed, even when despair knocks on your door, and it seems as if the walls are closing in, when you rebuke that demon and call up ***Jehovah Gibbor***, you have a newfound revelation in your victory in *Him* who told you that the battle belonged to *Him*. When sickness tries to bind you with the torment of death, even death has to bow down to *Yahweh* (2 Tim 1:7).

When you find yourself in a financial crisis, *Jehovah Chayil*, *God of wealth*, comes in and knocks down every limitation that blocks your path. There is a limitless flow in the spiritual realm, as *El Shaddai* blesses you with above, beyond and exceeding anything you could ever ask or desire. Remember, every knee must bow, and every tongue must confess that *He* is *Lord*; even the devourer bows down and loosens your money (Eph 3:20).

There is power in the name of *Jesus*. Faith and hope rise up in the midst of trials... in the center of tribulation. As you ascend in the spirit of the miraculous, you begin to understand that cloud by day and that fire by night, because you are more than a conqueror in *Christ*. You look at your feet that carried you across the Red Sea; you—yes, you—walked on dry land by the governing of the *Spirit* of the *living and true God*. You shall live and you shall not die because you have to declare the works of the *Most High* (Psa 118:17)!

El Elyon, the *Most High God*, the first cause of everything; the originator, the merciful *God*, the faithful *God*, the highest *Sovereign* of the Heavens and the Earth... for *He* is truth, justice, righteousness, and perfection (1 Chr 29:11)! *He* is *El Elyon*!

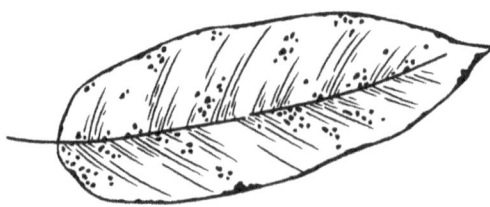

Musings

What part of this 'Peace' stirred you and why?

_____
_____
_____
_____
_____
_____
_____

Meanderings

Did this 'Peace' trigger any particular memory and why?

_____
_____
_____
_____
_____
_____
_____

Meditations

What secret place will you allow **Jehovah Rapha** to minister to you as you ponder this 'Peace'?

Esteem

Isaiah 53:3

To esteem is to respect and admire, to value, to revere someone. *Father God*, I esteem *You* eternally. From the birthing of my first word to the ceasing of my last breath, I will esteem *You*, for *You* are greatly to be praised.

I enthusiastically esteem *You*, *Elohim*, knowing that in the beginning, *God*, *You* created me for *Your* great pleasure... to learn of *You* intimately and intentionally. I am ever on *Your* mind. Just as *You* know each star and their proper placement and position, their uprisings and down-sitting. *You* know, and are my *Genesis* to my *Revelation*, my *Alpha* to my *Omega*. *You* are my best-selling author. I esteem *You* for thinking me worthy of authoring my destiny, of prospering my way and shielding me from harm, because even in the storm, *You* reign supreme as my vindicator, and my victory! I esteem *You* as I trust *You* explicitly. My faith is not in my sight or what's in my hand, but in *You*, of *whom* all things were made, and all things consist (Gen 1:1; Heb 12:2; Jer 29:11; Col 1:16,17).

I graciously clap my hands as I esteem *You*, for how excellent are all of *Your* ways (Psa 47:1).

I humbly bow my head as I esteem *You*, for there is none greater than *You*. It is indeed an honor and privilege to be in *Your* presence (Mic 6:6)!

I dutifully bend my knees as I esteem *You* before *Your* throne of grace; for there was a great price of grace paid for me to approach *Your* throne (Eph 3:14). I esteem *You* because I am sealed by the *Holy Spirit* (Eph 1:13). Thank *You*, *Jesus*, for being my *Redeemer*, my *Sanctifier*, my *Purifier*, my *Refiner*, and my *Atoning Sacrifice* (1 John 2:2).

In ultimate praise, I esteem *You* as I stomp my feet as the glory of the *Most High* provokes me to move and glorify *You* in a joyful dance with *You*, as my *Father* (Psa 30:11).

My worship is totally inclined to esteem *You*, for *You* are *Adonai*, unchanging and purposeful in that I revere *You* as *Jehovah Jireh*. Believing and speaking of the signs, miracles and wonders of *You* as the *Father* of glory (Eph 1:17).

Abba Father sent *His* only begotten *Son* in whom *He* was well pleased to sacrifice *HIS* life. *He* who was without sin became sin that we, *His* beloved, might have the abundance of eternal life in *Him*. Though *He* was rejected by those *He* came to save, *He* never faltered from the task set before *Him*. *He* shed *His* unblemished blood, for one, for all; yet *He* was esteemed not (Isa 53:3)!

How privileged are blood-washed believers today who can learn of *Him* afresh with each new sunrise as *He* gifts us with new mercies (Lam 3:22, 23).

Even when we who know *Him* as the *Resurrected Christ* still fall short and esteem *Him* not, rejecting *Him* for worldly lusts and desires of the flesh, we are continuously welcomed as *His* beloved. *His* love is unconditional. *He* is *Adonai*. As *His* beloved, by faith in our hearts, being rooted, grounded in love, joined together as *His* saints, we may be able to comprehend the breadth, length, depth and height, to intimately and intentionally commune with *Christ*. This relationship will consistently grow, and develop beyond our humanistic knowledge, yet we will be filled with all the fullness of *God* (Eph 3:18). *He* is a purposeful *Elohim*.

Count it all joy, and reverently esteem *Him*, to *whom* all the honor, all the glory, and all the praises are due (James 1:2)! *He* is worthy!

Abba Father, which art in heaven, hallowed be thy most *Holy Name*! We, your children, esteem *You* in all of *Your* reverential glory for *You* are wonderful! *You* are excellent! *You* are mighty! *You* are power! *You* are strength! *You* are all-knowing! *You* are all-wise! *You* are long-suffering! *You* are peace! *You* are ever-abiding! *You* are near! *You* are healer! *You* are a protector! *You* are a shield! *You* are the sun! *You* are shelter! *You* are magnificent! *You* are omnipotent! *You* are victorious! *You* are perfection to the utmost parts of the world! *You* are the *all in all*! We, *Your* children, esteem *You* to the utmost! Glory be to the *living and true God*!

Musings

What part of this 'Peace' stirred you and why?

_____
_____
_____
_____
_____
_____

Meanderings

Did this 'Peace' trigger any particular memory and why?

_____
_____
_____
_____
_____
_____

Meditations

What secret place will you allow **Jehovah Rapha** to minister to you as you ponder this 'Peace'?

Excited

Proverbs 13:25

Do you ever get excited at the thought of the expectation that comes with the *Word of* **God** (Heb 11:6)? To be excited is defined as being very enthusiastic or eager.

Some people get excited about seeing a loved one.

Some people get excited about getting a desired job.

Some people get excited over their favorite meal or dessert.

Some people get excited about getting married to the love of their life.

Some people get excited at the arrival of their 1st baby or grandbaby.

Some people get excited about getting their dream home.

Some people get excited about getting their luxury vehicles.

Some people get excited over a Hermes Birken bag or a Louis Vuitton purse.

Some people get excited at receiving a beautiful pair of red bottom shoes.

Some people get excited about receiving a beautiful diamond ring.

Some people get excited at receiving a good report from the doctor.

Some people get excited at witnessing their answered prayer.

There are so many things to get excited about, whether they are superficial or significant; still, we find ourselves excited.

The *Word of God* says when I was a child I acted like a child, I thought as a child, but when I grew up and I had to look back over my life, I had to think things through; I found that the veil that was over my eyes was removed (1 Cor 13:11).

I wake up with the thought that I have another opportunity to ingest the *Word of God* (Eze 3:1).

Another day's journey equalizes another infusion of the *Word of God* (Josh 1:8). The *Word of God* takes the stony heart and makes it flesh. *He* reconstructs my thoughts, my being, and I become rooted in the immovable *Word of God* (Eze 36:26, 27)! When you get excited in a fresh *Word of God* knowing beyond a shadow of a doubt that this is a *Word* from the *Most High* and you are in the proper posture to receive it, that is something to get excited about.

Excited about another opportunity to follow the *Word* to higher ground as you find refuge from the storm, sitting under the shadow of the *Almighty* (Isa 91:1).

Excited about the honor and the glory that you find in the *Word of God* as you seek *His* face evermore (Psa 105:4).

Revelation comes with the knowledge that in all of our accomplishments, these are blessings from on high, for *He* heard your cry, *He* honored your petition and gave you the desires of your heart. Yet as exciting as they are/were, nothing is as fulfilling as the *Word of God* (John 1:1). *Jesus* told the people, "Don't work for food that perishes, but for food that endures and leads to eternal life" (John 6:27). There is an excitement, an exuberance, in each new dawn in partaking of our daily bread, the *Word of God*. It's fresh and made especially for you. It's reverential, revelatory, and relevant in the lives of all believers without regard to who you are or where you are in your walk with *Christ*, for *God* has no respect of person (Eph 6:9).

Like the woman at the well, *He* will meet you where you are, and upon the introduction to *His* amazing grace and bountiful mercy, there will be a transfiguration of your life, because you cannot experience *Him* and be unchanged (John 4:7-29).

Please know that there is no pit too deep or dark or even too dangerous that *He* won't come and redeem you. There is no mountain too high that *He* won't reach down and rescue you, for *He* is the *Redeemer* of the living and the dead in *Christ* (Luke 4:18; Gal 3:13; Rom 8:38, 39). Excitement causes you to not only eat the 'bread of heaven' but to thirst for righteousness that is plentiful in the *Word of God,* and there is a spiritual infilling that allows the seeker to be filled with the *Living Water* (Matt 5:6). The *Word of God* guides us to not seek the things we see or desire with our natural eyes, for they are temporal, but to seek the unseen in the spirit because this is of the *Eternal Spirit*, from which *Abba Father* exposes with power and might and grace to all who will delve deeper into *His inexhaustible Word* (2 Cor 4:18). Remember, heaven and earth will pass away, but the *Word of God* shall remain (Matt 24:35). My prayer for you and me today is that we find joy, peace and love within the excitement of the *Word of God* (Gen 1:1; John 1:1).

#KINGDOMPEACES

Musings

What part of this 'Peace' stirred you and why?

_____
_____
_____
_____
_____
_____

Meanderings

Did this 'Peace' trigger any particular memory and why?

_____
_____
_____
_____
_____
_____
_____

Meditations

What secret place will you allow **Jehovah Rapha** to minister to you as you ponder this 'Peace'?

Exclusivity

John 16:27

It's not my desire to be in a causal relationship with **You**. But my aspiration is to be devoted and exclusive to **You** alone. No matter what season I encounter, I don't want to do it without **You**. For I know **You** to be **Jehovah Jireh** in season as well as out of season.

I know **You** rain on the obedient as well as the disobedient (Matt 5:45). I know that **You** have a plan for the haves as well as the have nots. I find great joy in seeking **You** diligently to acknowledge **You** in all of my ways that my steps may be ordered and my path directed by the **Maestro** of my destiny (1 Sam 2:9). The **Lyricist** of my melody is orchestrated for me alone with the purest of intentions.

The exclusivity that I find in **You** fills me with an unsurpassed peace (Phil 4:7). My posture of prayer and worship is heightened with each revelatory moment shared between **You** and me. In the past, I would continuously be distracted from spending time with **You**. Busyness in my daily ordeals would steal my plans to find that space in **You** (Prov 4:25). Frustration would kill my devotion and leave me depleted. Chasing the joy of **Your** strength, I'd wander from the original plan and become overwhelmed with weariness. Completely clueless to the method of this madness called life, I'd pray for instruction and discipline. Then one day I finally took a seat in a quiet space, no noise at all... just **You** and me. In the midst of that special moment in time, I felt **You** cover me with an inexplicable calmness; I was enveloped with **Your** unconditional love (Lam 3:25).

In this moment, tears race down my face. I feel a fresh awakening that signifies a renewal of my being. I look to the heavens because I know that *You* have literally touched me, and I see the brightest red bird sit in the middle of the street looking at me. With holy  hands, I worship *You* in honesty and truth (John 4:23). I find myself in a covenant relationship with my forever true love! The *lover of my soul* because *You* blow my mind in amazement and awe.

I want to be *Yours* only forever — all the days of my life. I desire what *You* would have for me all of the days *You* have ordained for me in this life and that which is to come in eternity. *Your* love makes me brand new, and it purifies the *spirit of You* in me (Psa 51:2). The exclusivity that I yearn for can only be satisfied by *You* (Psa 17:15).

Thank *You*, *Father*, that we can be in divine covenant and I don't have to worry about *You* hurting me or neglecting me (1 Chr 16:34). *Your* love is so broad that I have no fear of being cheated on because of the love *You* designed just for me... *You* give the same love to the lady who may sit beside me, and she too is satisfied with *Your* unconditional love (Psa 117:2). *You* don't differentiate. *Your* abundance manifests and fulfills the need. I realize that *You* are truly righteous and *You* love the same. Thank *You* for being mighty, powerful, omnipotent, kind, loving, forgiving, patient, long-suffering, generous, gracious, and merciful.

Thank *You* for granting my heart's desire to be exclusive with *You* as my soul mate (Psa 37:4)! Greater is *You*, *Abba Father* that is in me (1 John 4:4)! Thank *You* for being the keeper of my very being (Acts 17:28)! Thank *You* for knowing my name, allowing me to abide in *You*, *Your* word abiding in me and residing in me as *Your* temple and *Your* habitation (John 15:4). Thank *You* for this relationship that is intimately exclusive... me and *You*... *You* and me.

Musings

What part of this 'Peace' stirred you and why?

_____
_____
_____
_____
_____
_____
_____

Meanderings

Did this 'Peace' trigger any particular memory and why?

_____
_____
_____
_____
_____
_____
_____
_____

Meditations

What secret place will you allow **Jehovah Rapha** to minister to you as you ponder this 'Peace'?

Folly

James 4:17

Remember, as a kid, when we heard about Lot's plight in life, when he had to evacuate the premises immediately — all that he had accrued. He had to leave his street creds, his life of comfort, his friends (whether they were flawed or fluffed), his home, and he had no time to pack (Gen 19:1-26).

Instruction from **Father** informs us to love not the world; nor the things that are in the world (1 John 2:15). We acknowledge that friendship with the world makes us an enemy to **God** (James 4:4). There was an urgency placed upon the shoulders of Lot — he had to choose that day whom he would serve, **God** or mammon. Lot had to make a life-altering choice (Josh 24:15; Luke 16:13).

To obey is better than to sacrifice, because rebellion is as the sin of witchcraft, and stubbornness is as iniquity and idolatry (1 Sam 15:22, 23). That's the *Word*.

One of the most memorable events of Lot's historic chapter in the Bible was the fate of his wife; her folly (foolishness), she made the mistake of looking back in open disobedience... a pillar of salt she became. She lost her life because she was a slave to her flesh, to the lust for earthly things that held no relevance. Folly at its finest, with her picture attached to it.

The 'return' can be an expensive price to pay, and many times people fail to count the cost. There is a price for everything. Whether you pay it or someone else has to pay it for you, there is still a cost.

The cost of sin and salvation was paid in full when **Yeshua** gave **His** life. Our **Father** which art in heaven gave **His** only begotten **Son** that we who believe would have everlasting life in **Christ** (John 3:16). There is growth in our relationship with **Elohim** when we submit by the transformation of our minds to the perfecting that is in **Christ** (Rom 12:2).

When we look back with lustful eyes at what we were delivered from, we are rebuking **Elohim**; we are forsaking our deliverance. Just as in the scripture where it says: the dog is turned to his own vomit again; and the sow that was washed to her wallowing in the mire (2 Pet 2:22). A fool repeats his folly (Prov 26:11).

Why? Because it's as fool's gold — it glitters and deceives, and it provides us with a familiarity that will cause self-destruction if we aren't careful.

There are many encounters on this journey called life, times, that we seek **God** with diligence and reverence and beseech **Him** for many things. It may be for children, for spouses, for parents, for employment, for money, for healing, for deliverance from addictions (seen and unseen, acknowledged and unacknowledged). Whatever it may be, we know that **He** holds the answer within **His** mighty righteous hand (James 4:16). We believe that **God** is able to make all grace abound toward us; that we, having sufficiency in all things, may abound to every good work for the *Glory of God* (2 Cor 9:8)!

Yet many times when we read the *Word of God*, we find ourselves feeling exempt from the many pitfalls we witness in others who have subjected themselves to within the 66 chapters of the *World's Best-Selling* book. Case in point: Lot's Wife. We feel as if she was a fool, but how many of us can truthfully say that we would not hesitate or question **El Shaddai** if **He** instructed us to leave all that **He** had blessed us with? Although we know what we have is not because we have been so good, or even deserved the goodness of the **Most High**, but could you, would you be able to truly walk away without a second glance (James 1:17)? Because we are reading about what once was, we sometimes feel as if we are above reproach, and it's so easy to say that we wouldn't have fallen too. We crucify Eve, yet how many times a day do we eat that fruit that the prince of this world presents to us? How many times have we chosen mates that we know were not our *God*-sent mate and allowed them to lead us into places of darkness? We deem Adam as weak when we too are weak to the flesh. We miss the mark of excellence because of our slave mentality to what feels good, looks good, and we think will be good to us and for us (Rom 7:14-17).

When we receive the *Good News* in the fullness of **Father God**, the *all in all*, the fullness of time, we can glory in the divine revelation that in *Him* there is no failure (Josh 21:45). As we grow in relationship with *Elohim*, as we submit to *Jehovah Rohi*, as we glorify *El Shaddai*, as we revere *El Elyon*, *El Emuwnah*, the peace that surpasses all understanding will assail our senses, and we will hurriedly kneel and obey *His* command, counting it a joy and a privilege to be *His* offspring, knowing that *He* works all things unto perfection that *He* strategically assigns to our designated plight on this side of glory! We intentionally choose *Yeshua*, for *He* is *God* all by *Himself*! We worship the *Father* of lights, with which there is no variation. *He* is unchanging! Yesterday's folly has no power, no hold over us. *He* is *God*, *He* is *God*, *He* is *God*.

#KINGDOMPEACES

Musings

What part of this 'Peace' stirred you and why?

_____
_____
_____
_____
_____
_____
_____

Meanderings

Did this 'Peace' trigger any particular memory and why?

_____
_____
_____
_____
_____
_____
_____

Meditations

What secret place will you allow **Jehovah Rapha** to minister to you as you ponder this 'Peace'?

Further

2 Timothy 2:13

Loss of a loved one, loss of a lifestyle, loss of a dream, loss of income, loss of health — loss is the decrease of something. In the residue of loss, sometimes it pushes you to a place that is quiet. It's welcoming and more than anything, it feels safe. The darkness lulls you into a deceptive calm that wraps strong arms around you, and once you're enfolded into its grasp, you rest in it — in the arms of a stronghold.

Have you ever discovered that every welcoming emotion isn't necessarily welcoming you for your good? That everything that appears good, speaks of goodness, gives the faulty appearance of good; yet when light overcomes darkness, and the truth has reared its vicious head, you're stuck looking star-struck, because you just got duped by the false angel of light (2 Cor 11:14). Light and darkness can't abide in the same place (2 Cor 6:14). This place of oppression is possessive and will beckon you to delve too far and to abide too long in reclusiveness. In this place there is no hope, no peace, no joy, no love, no kindness, no compassion — only contempt, unforgiveness, bitterness, accusations, pity, envy, jealousy, malice, hopelessness, and so many other negative markers that will taunt you as you are beaten down mentally in believing the lie that there is no escape for you.

Hurt and disappointment can take you to a place so lonesome that you have no desire to believe, trust or even dream anymore. Sometimes in our disobedience, we delve further than we were sent, and we stayed much longer than we were meant to stay. This place is not *God* ordained. *God* has no desire for *His* children to dwell in depression; for

He promised that every valley would be filled (Isa 40:4). *He* purposed that we would have the desires of our hearts, but it has a condition (Psa 37:4). Just as *He* told the blind men, 'Be it unto you according to your faith,' *He's* unchanging, as is *His* Living Word (Matt 9:29). Know that *He* has no respect of person (Rom 2:11).

We have to be like Lazarus and come forth and be loosed from our grave clothes (John 11:43-44). Whatever the provocation that lured you into bondage, you have to recognize the trigger and disable it. How so? By rejecting the allure of the darkness, because you are not to walk in the counsel of the wicked, but to find delight in the *law of the Lord*, by meditating on *His* Word, day and night. Envision yourself as a well-watered tree that is fertilized with the *Living Water* yielding fruit in season (Psa 1:1-3).

Rejoice in the *Lord*, for *He* is your strength (Neh 8:10)! Find your dwelling place in *El Emuwnah* for *He* remains faithful (2 Tim 2:13)! Allow *Him* to be your resting place, the *Alpha* and the *Omega*. *Jesus Christ*, our *Redeemer*, came, that we might have life in abundance; that we'd walk in the anointing of *His Amazing Grace* and the manifestation of the power of the *Holy Spirit* that will resonate of the wisdom of *Elohim*. If you long for habitation, may you find your resting place under the shadow of *His* wings (Psa 17:8). Let your desires be known only in the presence of the *Master*, the *living and true God*! If you desire 'further', if you yearn for 'deeper', heed the voice of *Jehovah Rohi* to lead you. May your 'further' be in *Him* whose love for you has no boundaries!

Musings

What part of this 'Peace' stirred you and why?

_____
_____
_____
_____
_____
_____

Meanderings

Did this 'Peace' trigger any particular memory and why?

_____
_____
_____
_____
_____
_____
_____

Meditations

What secret place will you allow **Jehovah Rapha** to minister to you as you ponder this 'Peace'?

Good

James 4:17

Thank *You*, *Lord*, for this day! Thank *You*, *Lord*, for awakening us to another unpromised day! Thank *You*, *Lord*, for being a *promise-keeper* and a *covenant-keeping God*! Thank *You*, *Father*, for seeing fit to call our names and most of all, *Father*, for *always* remembering us when sometimes people forget about us, overlook us, or ostracize us (Isa 43:1). We are too often judged by a jury of 12 or carried by 6, but *You* are the ultimate *Judge*, the *Justifier* as well as the *Purifier*!

Your ways are perfect. We discover this revelation each time we sit at *Your* feet and seek *Your* teaching from Genesis to Revelation. It's free (2 Tim 2:15).

Thank *You*, *Father*, for being such a good *Father* that gives good gifts. For every good and perfect gift comes from *Abba Father* which art in heaven (James 1:17)! For if our earthly father knows how to give good gifts, how much more than our *Heavenly Father* that sits in heaven on *His* throne and looks low on the earth, which is *His* footstool (Luke 11:11-13; Acts 7:49). *Lord*, *You* called us into being. *You* assigned us tasks that we could accomplish and tests that we could overcome.

We speak in past tense because once we settle into *Jesus Christ*, it has already been done! *Jesus* declared, *'It Is Finished'* (John 19:30**)**. *Jesus Christ* did it all for us. It's only in *Him* that we discover the accomplishments of perfection! The overcomer spirit resides in the bosom of *Chris*t. *His* love overcomes a multitude of sins unconditionally

(1 Pet 4:8). *His* love cleanses us of all unrighteousness as we accept *Him* as *Jehovah Tsidkenu*. *His* love took our sins, sorrows, trials, tribulations, burdens, and even our residue. *He* voluntarily, not of coercion, but of grace, took it all just for you, me, us, and *He* left it all on the *Cross at Calvary* (Col 2:13-15). *His* unblemished blood purified every stain and every stench (Isa 1:18).

His blood soothed every wail, every cry, every place of hurt. *His* blood did that unquestionably! *His* blood illuminated every dark place, every hidden vein of evil, every place of shame, every shallow ground. *His* blood radiated the brilliance of redemption that **only** the *Lamb of God* could fulfill (John 8:12).

He is the only *One* that can make the bad good (Gen 50:20). *He* is the good that is birthed from every bad pregnancy. The *Lord* hath made all things for *Himself*: yea, even the wicked for the day of evil (Prov 16:4). *He* assured us that what the enemy meant for evil, *He* will use it for good (Gen 50:20). *He* further affirms *His* divine intentions with the glorious revelation that **all** things work together for the good to them that love *God* and are called according to *His* purpose (Rom 8:28). *He* is the only one that takes your darkest day and lightens it with a divine experience that will catapult you on that path of 'greater' that you calculated impossible (John 11:9-11).

Elohim is the *Good Father!* *He* is the *Good Shepherd*, *Jehovah Rohi*, for in *Him* there is no insufficiency (Psa 23:1). *He* is the goodness and mercy of the *Lord*, for *He* is *God* by *Himself*. *He* needs you for nothing, not even a piece of bread (Psa 5:12). *He* is the corrector and the one who offers reproof for *He* knows the purposes and plans *He* has for you. *He* knows the prosperity that *He* has assigned to you before you were formed in your mother's womb (Jer 29:11; Jer 1:5). *He* knows when you shall be beguiled into an off-season and when you will be led in season to overflow and excess. *He* knows the good, *He* sees the bad, yet only *He* can turn water into wine.

He'll take the craving, the power of addiction, and replace your taste for destruction to that of empowerment so much so that you shall hunger and thirst for righteousness (Matt 5:6). What one man calls worthless; ***He*** deems rich in ***His*** glory! ***He*** is the Divine Orchestrator! ***He*** is grand in ***His Omnipotence*** for ***He*** never leaves nor forsakes you as you rest in ***Jehovah Shammah***! ***He*** is a *Good **Father*** that is ever-abiding even in your treacherous spaces of time. The times when shame overshadows you, ***He's*** that last thread of hope that whispers that ***He'll*** take the pain away (Psa 46:1,11). You only have to accept ***Him*** and heed the voice of the ***Most High*** (Matt 11:15). ***He's*** good and ***He's*** good always, even until the end of time! Suffer the bad for the good, for the ***Revealer of Truth*** is indeed good for ***He*** is the living and the true ***God*** (1 Pet 3:17). ***He*** is good!

Musings

What part of this 'Peace' stirred you and why?

_____
_____
_____
_____
_____
_____
_____

Meanderings

Did this 'Peace' trigger any particular memory and why?

_____
_____
_____
_____
_____
_____
_____

Meditations

What secret place will you allow **Jehovah Rapha** to minister to you as you ponder this 'Peace'?

Grateful

Ephesians 5:20

I am always so amazed when I see the righteous hand of **God** in my life. I believe that I am one of **His** chosen vessels. I believe that the favor of the **Most High** is upon me and all of my assignments. I am so grateful to have the privilege to seek **Him** while **He** may be found. I am so grateful that **He** is my **Deliverer** (Psa 18:2)! I am so grateful that **He** is my **God**, **Mighty in Battle**, and that I can entrust every one of my cares unto **Him**, that I have the honor of casting them at **His** perfect feet. **He** doesn't frown upon me in my weaknesses, my flaws, my humanity; but **He** weeps when *I am* broken, and **He** absorbs my wails of despair for **He** is **Jehovah Gibbor** (1 Pet 5:7; Psa 24:8). **His** love is so pure that **He** consecrates that which was filthy with **His** blood and takes the stain of my sins and cleanses me of all unrighteousness (Isa 1:18). **He** hears the simplicity of my requests that I complexify in my human sight, the things that I magnify in unbelief, and still, **He** smiles because there is absolutely nothing that is too hard for **Elohim**, for in weakness **He** is strong (Matt 19:26).

What a privilege to serve the **One** that sits high in heaven on **His** throne and looks so low, for the earth is **His** footstool (Isa 66:1). **He** looks upon man in all his iniquity, perversion, and malice, and still, **He** sees the good, for **He** knows **His** plans and purposes in **His** creation (Jer 29:11). **He** created man in **His** supreme image and bestowed power, authority, and dominion upon **His** image (Gen 1:26). Psalm 8 says, "*What is man, that* **He** *is mindful of him?*" There is honor in knowing that in all of man's evil and wickedness, in man's rebelliousness, **Abba Father** still reserves a ram in the bush to supply every need according to *His* limitless riches in glory; the ram is to serve as atonement for man's transgressions (Phil 4:19).

There is honor in *Jehovah Rohi*, in the magnification that sent the unblemished **Lamb of God** in *His* perfection as a sacrifice for all men, not a select sector, but for all men — unbelievers as well as believers. Despite the obvious rejection of the unbeliever, *He* still shed *His* unblemished blood for them. **Abba Father** sent *His Son*, with dominion and power to exemplify servitude, humility, meekness — not weakness, not flaws, not fearfulness, not dishonor — but glory and *His* omnipotent honor.

He promised that the **Messiah's** coming would rectify the wrong… that the *Angel of the Lord* would make every crooked path straight. *He* promised that *His* beloved *Son* in whom *He* is well pleased would move the looming obstacles as *He* brings the hill and the mountain low. The tears shed in the sorrowful valley of Baca would turn like the sun from weeping and wailing to praises and rejoicing as the **Father of Compassion** replenishes every valley with *His* all-consuming love. The intolerable places, those rough patches in life, the places where man would grow weary in well doing, where man would begin to lose hope, *He* promised as our *Hope of Glory*, that *He* would smoothen it out effortlessly because there is a harvest for those that pursue peace with passion and press toward the mark of the high calling in **Christ** (Isa 40:4; Col 1:27; Phil 3:14). Greater is *He* that is in you than he that is in the world (1 John 4:4). For many are the afflictions of the righteous but the **Lord** delivers him of them all (Psa 34:19)! Glory be to our **Redeemer** for how excellent are *His* ways! Glory be to the **Most High**!

Musings

What part of this 'Peace' stirred you and why?

_____
_____
_____
_____
_____
_____

Meanderings

Did this 'Peace' trigger any particular memory and why?

_____
_____
_____
_____
_____
_____

Meditations

What secret place will you allow **Jehovah Rapha** to minister to you as you ponder this 'Peace'?

Greetings

Numbers 6:23-27

Greetings, Beloved of the *Most High*! Greetings to the one that seeks the *One* each and every day knowing that *He* alone is *the Author* and *Finisher* of your faith (Heb 12:2). *He's* so gracious and *His* love is so uninhibited and unrestrictive that *He* will accept your mustard seed of faith (Matt 17:20). Your mustard seed will not place you at the back of the line for *He* promised that you would be first and not last. *He* promised that you would be above and not beneath (Deut 28:13).

So how does *Elohim*, Our *Creator*, accept our very least in exchange for *His* very best? *He* is the *Potter* (Isa 64:8). *He* is the *Master*. *He* is the *Author* and *He* is the *Finisher*! *He* has dealt to every man a measure of faith (Rom 12:3).

May *Jehovah Shalom* meet and greet you this morning with a 'peace be still' in this tumultuous storm that you are weathering. The waves seem to overlap your voyage and you've cried for help. You ask *HIM* if *He* heard you? Does *He* even care that you may die in this storm (Mark 4:35-41)? What good are you and your works from the grave (Isa 38:18)? And in the twinkling of an eye, *He* answers.

Jehovah Shalom met you where you were and calmed every difficult place. Did they actually dissolve? Not all of them, but *He* wrapped you in a peace that surpassed understanding. You experienced *His* peace, which is not the peace that the world offers, but a peace that transcends time, space, and limitations, even your harrowing circumstances (Phil 4:7).

He instructs us to seek *Him* while *He* may be found, and call upon *Him* while *He* is near (Isa 55:6). Thus, the purpose for accepting the invitation. The purpose for praising *Him* while we are in the storms, in the trials and, in the persecution. It's the glory of these moments that we gain an understanding of the need to humble ourselves and look to the hills from whence cometh our help. Knowing and believing that all of our help comes from the *Lord* (Psa 121:1). *He* is worthy to be praised!

The purpose of "Thanking *Him*" for these hard places is because, in these forsaken places, we meet *Jehovah Shalom*. It's in the testimony that you realize how *He* washed you afresh with *His* peace. *He* touched you in a special place and cleansed you from the impurities of hurt, harm, and danger with *His* pure love that overcomes all the elements of life in this world of darkness (John 16:33).

You were purified with the *Light of the World! Jehovah M'Kaddesh* swept in and sanctified you in this place and set you apart. You had to find solace at the pinnacle of the mountain and allow *Jehovah Tsidkenu* to cleanse you of all iniquities and transgressions. You released the spirit of disobedience in exchange for the righteousness of *Jesus Christ*. You welcomed *Him* to inhabit you (Acts 26:15-18). You glorify *His indwelling Spirit* and follow *Jehovah Rohi* to lead, guide, direct and instruct you. You hunger and thirst for the *Good Shepherd* (John 7:37). You sit under the tutelage of *Adonai*, being blessed with the revelation that *He* is the same and that *His* love is ever-abiding and unchanging. *His* love neither increases nor decreases; *He* just seeks that you decrease that *He* might increase (John 3:30). For greater is *He* that is in you than he that is in the world (1 John 4:4).

May you further be greeted by *Jehovah Jireh* as you find sufficiency in *His* grace upon the understanding that *He* and only *He*, your *Father of Glory*, provides every last one of your needs according to *His* limitless riches in glory (Phil 4:19).

Remember, *He* knows your story and has given you provision because *He* has already prepared the table before you. Take your rightful seat as a *Son of God*, as a joint heir of *Christ*, as an heir of the *Most High* (Rom 8:16,17). Glorify *El Shaddai*, *God* Almighty of blessings as your cup runneth over (Psa 23:5)! Lift up holy hands toward the open heaven in expectation (Mal 3:10).

In the midst of this holy moment, you accept your victory, *His* banner, *His* standard, *His* unconditional love blankets you in the midst of the cruelties of this world. Cruelties that are of no effect because you dwell in the secret place of the *Most High*. Yes, you as a believer and of a chosen generation reside in Goshen (Psa 91:1; Gen 45:10, 11). *He* will hide you under the shadow of *His* wings as *He* is exalted as your place of refuge (Psa 91:1)! *Jehovah Nissi* just overshadowed you so swiftly that you almost missed *His* greeting; *He* moves graciously.

As you accept this victory in *Jehovah Gibbor*, the *Lord God*, an unforeseen enemy ensues as your body is attacked (Psa 34:19). And you feel as if *God* is laughing, as if you are the butt of a bad joke. What just happened? You were in an elevated place in *Him*. *Abba Father* does indeed laugh at the antics of the prince of darkness (Psa 37:12,13). *Jehovah Gibbor* is mighty, the joy of the *Lord* is your strength and *He* has yet another opportunity to introduce *His* multi-faceted character as *Jehovah Rapha*, *He* who stands guard over you (Neh 8:10; Psa 18:1,2). *Jehovah Rapha* takes residence as your gatekeeper, and *He* blesses you with mercy that makes even the bitter experiences sweet (Exod 15:22-27).

Abba Father sent *His* prized possession for you. This attack was nailed to the cross, and *His Word* left it there (1 Pet 2:24). That's why *He* commands you to take up your sickbed and walk (John 5:8)! The healing covered you before it manifested! *He* is well able — above, beyond, and exceeding (Eph 3:20,21)! As you bow down to *Him* who is worthy to be praised, *El Elyon*, the *Everlasting God* greets you with a kiss as *His* beloved, *His* masterpiece that *He* orchestrated fearfully and wonderfully, *His* Creation (Psa 139:14). *He* created you in faithfulness, in truth, in righteousness, and perfection. Completed in *His* greatest revelation — *Jesus*. *Jehovah Chayil*, our wealthy place adorns you with unfathomable riches! You're experiencing the fullness of *God*!

This meet and greet is iconic and unforgettable. It will be rendered the greatest for each and every manifestation of *His* appearance in our lives and the lives of our loved ones! We are cognizant of *His* ever-abiding presence and ability as *El Elyon* (Isa 43:2)! We bless *You El Roi*, for *You* neither slumber nor sleep, but *You* are mindful of our weaknesses, and we are grateful for *Your* power and might (Psa 121:4)!

Thank *You*, *Jehovah Shammah* for never leaving nor forsaking us even at the lowest place. Even in the valley of the shadow of death, *Your* abiding presence strengthens us because we know that *You* indeed are victory, power, honor, and glory (Rom 8:38,39)! We count it an honor and a privilege to call *You* our *Lord* and our *Savior*, our *Deliverer*, our *Messiah*! Hallelujah! Amen!

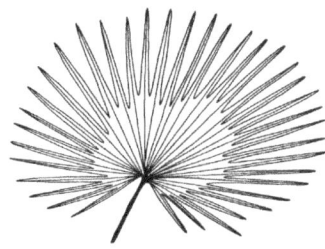

Musings

What part of this 'Peace' stirred you and why?

_____
_____
_____
_____
_____
_____

Meanderings

Did this 'Peace' trigger any particular memory and why?

_____
_____
_____
_____
_____
_____
_____

Meditations

What secret place will you allow **Jehovah Rapha** to minister to you as you ponder this 'Peace'?

Heads and Tails

Deuteronomy 28:13

There are two sides to a coin — the head and the tail. Up and down. Right and wrong. Winning and losing. There are two sides to a coin. Some people know the good side of you and some know the bad side. I heard a singer say that for a couple there is his side, her side, and the truth.

Jesus tells us, 'Sanctify through thy truth: Thy **Word** is truth' (John 17:17). We can experience many things in our lives. Some good. Some bad. Some bad we use for good. And some good we use for bad. It's in these life-altering instances that we get revelation and understanding that 'all things work together for the good of those who are called according to **His** purpose' (2 Tim 1:9).

God is not a wasteful **God**. **God** is a purposeful **God**. **God** ordains. **God** says that there shall be no lack or insufficiency (Judg 19:19). **God** purposes overflow in all of our lives. It's just the choices we make, if they be the heads or the tails. What you think on the longest becomes the strongest (Prov 23:7). What you invest in determines your lot. If you find yourself investing in the *Word of God*, you will find that you experience supernatural goodness. Even when the gates of hell open on you, they shall not prevail (Matt 16:18).

Thy **Word** is truth. Thy **Word** is faithful. Thy **Word** is without reproof. Thy **Word** is from Genesis to Revelation. Thy **Word** shall remain when heaven and earth pass away (Mark 13:31). Thy **Word** shall reign in the new heavens and the new earth.

Jesus became our new covenant. ***He*** is the gate. We receive all impartation from ***Father God*** through the gate (John 10:9). Whatever your lot may present, know that heads and tails — heads or tails — whatever you perceive, your perseverance will be determined by ***Elohim***. ***He*** does all things very well. Seek *Alpha and Omega* in season and out of season. Everlasting ***God, El Elyon*** (Gen 21:33).

Abba desires that you receive the goodness of the ***Lord*** all the days of your life (Psa 23:6). Seek *Alpha and Omega*, for the ***Lord*** is good to those that wait for ***Him***, to the soul that trusts ***Him*** (Lam 3:25). Instead of thinking of the flip side of the coin, just declare: The ***Lord*** is my portion, and place all of your hope in ***Him*** (Lam 3:24). For ***He*** is the ***Sovereign Ruler, El Elyon*** (Gen 21:33).

Musings

What part of this 'Peace' stirred you and why?

_____
_____
_____
_____
_____
_____

Meanderings

Did this 'Peace' trigger any particular memory and why?

_____
_____
_____
_____
_____
_____
_____

Meditations

What secret place will you allow **Jehovah Rapha** to minister to you as you ponder this 'Peace'?

Holy Spirit

John 14:26

The *Holy Spirit* is of the Divine *Trinity* — all separate yet, one. I am discovering my best friend, my BFFFFFF. The *Holy Spirit* is the 'wind beneath my wings.' The *Holy Spirit* is the friend that I have overlooked my entire life, taking *Him* for granted. *He* has been there for me when I wanted to give up, reminding me just who my *Father* is. *He* whispers sweet nothings to me, encourages me, and brings to my remembrance scripture that I have read during my past bible study, and that applies to my current situations and circumstances (John 14:26).

The *Holy Spirit* tells me that I have great purpose. *He* coaxes me to continue to do good when I grow weary in being kind (Gal 6:9). *He* has been the friend that calms my raging sea down, when I probably should have lost my mind (Isa 26:3). *He* has been the friend that comforts me in my wilderness experiences. *He* is that small voice in the still of the night. *He* has been that friend that I counted on and didn't even recall *His* name or thank *Him* for supporting me after a trying experience (John 15:15).

He has been that friend that I consistently take for granted. *He* has been my hero. When I received my shine, *He* remained in the shadows, never leaving me nor forsaking me (Deut 31:5). *He* never called me out for overlooking *His* abiding presence.

He has always been my #1 cheerleader. *He* tells me what thus saith the *Lord*. *He* tells me that I am worthy when others say I am nothing (Zeph 3:17).

He tells me that I am a good thing when others perceive me as useless, an afterthought. *He* tells me of my inner beauty, and not to focus on the outer appearance, the shell (1 Pet 3:3,4). For

beauty is like a flower in the field. The grass withers and the flower fades (1 Pet 1:24).

He tells me to be still, be quiet, and to see the salvation of *God* (Exod 14:13).

He instructs me of each task at hand and assures me of the limitless grace that *Father* has ordained for me (Phil 4:13).

When I ponder my best friend, my heart rejoices and my mind muses over the seamless unity between *Elohim*, *Jesus Christ* and the *Holy Spirit* (2 Cor 13:14). Separate yet one! My *God* is awesome!! Yes, *He* is!

Musings

What part of this 'Peace' stirred you and why?

_____
_____
_____
_____
_____
_____

Meanderings

Did this 'Peace' trigger any particular memory and why?

_____
_____
_____
_____
_____
_____

Meditations

What secret place will you allow **Jehovah Rapha** to minister to you as you ponder this 'Peace'?

If

2 Chronicles 7:14

If I never shed a tear, I'd never understand the essence of the joy of the **Lord**. I would never appreciate a silly giggle, a heartfelt chuckle, or a laugh from the pits of my belly (Psa 56:8).

If I never felt down in my spirits, I'd never be cognizant of the lifting of my head by ***Abba Father*** (Psa 145:14).

If I never got angry, I'd never know that I possess self-control. I'd never know that I am more than a conqueror through **Chris**t which strengthens me (Eph 4:26; Rom 8:37).

If I had never been in the valley low, I would never know how to treasure being on the mountaintop (Luke 3:5).

If I had never been crucified by man, I'd never bear witness of the justification of ***Jesus Christ*** (Rom 10:11).

If you had never taken that route, you wouldn't have had that wreck and totaled your new car. If you had not had that wreck, you wouldn't be able to comprehend the righteous right hand of **God** that allowed you to testify that although a vehicle was demolished, you only had one scratch on your forehead. You would never have had the opportunity to know that not only is **God** a keeper when you didn't realize that you needed to be kept; but you'd proclaim that **He** is ***Jehovah Gibbor***, the **Lord God** that is indeed *mighty in battle*. You would have missed the opportunity to reacquaint yourself with ***El Shaddai*** on another level, as **He** blesses you above, beyond, and exceeding your wildest imagination.

It's only in the 'if I had never' or 'if you had never' that we come into the fulfillment of *God* as the *All in All*. It's in life-altering moments that we come in alignment with the understanding that what the devil meant for evil, the *All Powerful, Almighty, All Wise God*, flipped the script for our good (Gen 50:20). Even in the midst of our mess, when we, like the prodigal son, choose to wallow in the mud in disobedience, *God* is right there patiently waiting on us to allow *Him* to wash us afresh and cleanse us of not only the mud that is seen in the natural eye; but, to cleanse our wretchedness with the  blood of the most *Holy Lamb of God*, that we might become new creatures in *His* beloved *Son*, *Jesus*, the *Resurrected Christ* (1 John 1:9). If we had never sinned, we wouldn't need a *Savior*! 'Never' has purpose too. Praise God! I am Redeemed (Isa 44:22)!

Musings

What part of this 'Peace' stirred you and why?

_____
_____
_____
_____
_____
_____

Meanderings

Did this 'Peace' trigger any particular memory and why?

_____
_____
_____
_____
_____
_____
_____

Meditations

What secret place will you allow **Jehovah Rapha** to minister to you as you ponder this 'Peace'?

Imperfections

Philippians 1:6

Be ye therefore perfect, even as your **Father** which is in heaven is perfect (Matt 5:48). Be ye holy, for **I Am** holy (1 Pet 1:16). And be not conformed to this world; but be ye transformed by the renewing of your mind, that ye may prove what is that good and acceptable, and

perfect will of **God** (Rom 12:2). Herein is my **Father** glorified, that ye bear much fruit; so, shall you be **My** disciples (John 15:7,8).

Powerful commands from *the Almighty, All-Powerful* **God**, the **Everlasting God, El Elyon**, the **Merciful God**, the **Most High God**, the **Highest Sovereign** of the heavens and the earth. **Elohim, Creator** of the heavens and earth and fullness thereof. The **One** that calls the stars by name, one by one and not one of them is misplaced; they are numbered, they are never forgotten, they are used for purpose, they magnify the glory of the **Most High** (Psa 147:4)! O **Lord**, our **Lord**, how excellent is **Thy Name** in all the earth (Psa 8:1)!

What is man that **Thou** art mindful of him (Psa 8:4)? **Lord**, what is man that **Thou** takest knowledge of him? Our **Father** which art in heaven; hallowed be **Thy Name** (Matt 6:9)! As we sit back in awe at the magnificent work of this great **God** we serve, we honor **Him**, yes! We worship **Him**, yes! But we find ourselves intimidated because of our blatant blunders, our constant falling short of **His** glory (Rom 3:23)! Shortcomings in and out of season, of which the accuser never fails to rage about; he accuses you before you go to bed, and he points them out to you when you awake (Rev 12:10). Yet, as we learn to drown out his lies and accusations with repentance, worship and the inexhaustible *Word of God*, we sometimes find ourselves shrinking back because of the warfare that is in fervent battle inside of us. Worldly thinking disillusions us with the weightiness of sinfulness; the mindset that perfection is not our portion, when *He's* given us the *Word* which instructs and guides us into all holiness. Be holy because *I Am* holy (Lev 11:45). Let your mind be as the mind of *Christ* (Phil 2:5).

Jehovah Tsidkenu ushers us into a place of repentance, as *He* assures us that all of our transgressions have been nailed to the cross (Col 2:14). The price of our iniquities has been satisfied, and our receipt presented for all believers to witness in the *Resurrected Christ* that ascended into heaven to continue that perfect work *Elohim* began, which is being completed in *His* only begotten  *Son* (Phil 1:6)! Our *Mediator* that steadfastly ministers to us, for us and with us. Our reassurance, the *Holy Spirit*, *Jehovah Shammah*, our consistent companion. When we walk through the valley of the shadow of death, we have no fear; for *God* did not give us the spirit of fear. *He* gave us the spirit of power, the spirit of love, and praise *God*, the spirit of a sound mind (Psa 107:14; 2 Tim 1:7).

Let us not shy away from the teaching of *Jehovah M'Kaddesh*, for *He* sanctifies as *Jehovah Tsidkenu* validates our righteousness through our ransom, *Jesus Christ* (1 Tim 2:5-6). Because of *Jesus* applying *His* unblemished blood upon the mercy seat, we have the privilege to approach the altar; we have the ability to ascend to the *Holy of Holies* with a reverential boldness and ask *Father* to teach us of *His* way (Heb 4:16). *He* says if we walk not in the counsel of the ungodly, nor sit in the seat of the scornful, but if we meditate on *His* law, day and night, if we delight in *His* law, we will be blessed (Psa 1:1-2). *Jehovah Rohi*, our *Good Shepherd*, promises that *He* will instruct us and teach us the way that we should go. *He* promised that *He* would guide us because *He* would keep *His* eye on us (Psa 32:8)! *He* basks in the glory due to *Him* when we humble ourselves and meditate on *His* word early in the morning, late in the midnight hour, when we seek *His* direction. *His* instruction, for *He* is our *vindicator* (Heb 11:6). Our victory resides in the palm of *His* hand, the purpose of our asking *Him* to teach our hands to war and our fingers to fight (Psa 144:1). We should have no trepidation in following *His* perfect and divine direction, for *He* knows all things, and *He* does all things very well.

Our angels, that war for us, that minister to us, that guard us, that bear us up in their hands lest we should dash our foot against a stone, are in awe of *God's* unconditional love for mere man. Angels muse over *God's* strategies in *His* divine purpose in man as they witness the innumerable missteps of this flawed creation; yet *His* unfailing love and forgiveness (Heb 1:14).

Our *Father* wants us to learn of *Him* and *His* ways in that we will strive to be what *He* purposed when *He* created us — a direct image of *Himself* (Gen 1:26). *His* love in perfecting all that we misconstrue was in the being of the **Resurrected Christ** that came as an open display of *God's* irreversible love for *His* creation. *He* demonstrated that *He* is approachable because *He* is ever near (Psa 145:18). Does *He* chasten? What good father doesn't? Is it for our demise? Indeed, no (Heb 12:6)! Being chastened (punished) isn't enjoyable while it is happening — more often than not, it hurts. But afterwards, when we can see the end result, we experience a quiet growth in grace and character (Heb 12:11). For when *Father* chastens (punishes) you, it proves *His* love for you.

Allow *God* to train you, for *He* is doing what any loving father does for his children (Heb 12:6,7). Humility is our teacher and is the way into all knowledge. Glory in the privilege that we are being taught of *Him* every day that *He* purposefully calls our name into consciousness. For *His* thoughts are not our thoughts, nor our ways, *His* way; for as the heavens are higher than the earth, so are *His* ways above our ways and *His* thoughts than our thoughts (Isa 55:8,9).

Musings

What part of this 'Peace' stirred you and why?

_____
_____
_____
_____
_____
_____

Meanderings

Did this 'Peace' trigger any particular memory and why?

_____
_____
_____
_____
_____
_____

Meditations

What secret place will you allow **Jehovah Rapha** to minister to you as you ponder this 'Peace'?

_____
_____
_____
_____
_____
_____
_____
_____
_____
_____
_____
_____
_____
_____
_____

Keys

Revelation 3:7

Keys are a necessity with purpose, to exposure; most immediately, think of unlocking something hidden. Annual Women's Days are promoted with a theme which is indicative of a 'key point' that will intrigue the ladies, and is especially heightened with the disclosure of the 'keynote speaker.' Excitement is in the atmosphere with the expectation that they deliver a spectacular word that will unlock the hidden mystery that has plagued you for such a time as this. The time for delivery is at hand — upon acceptance of the keys.

These are the words of *Him* who is holy and true, who holds the *key of David*. What *He* opens no man can shut, and what *He* shuts no man can open (Rev 3:7). Our praise is in the knowledge that *Father* will bless whom *He* will bless, and *He* will curse whom *He* will curse. When *God* speaks, the angels hasten to perform *His* commands (Num 22:12; Psa 103:20).

Many times, life has beaten us down and we find ourselves in a prison that we inadvertently created. We tenaciously design towering walls with insurmountable pillars of circumstances. Some are painted as sicknesses that we can't overcome; some are marriages that are irreparable, whatever it may be, you find yourself bound in misery. Some are jobs that produce no hope as you continue to toddle down the same path with no advancement in sight. Some even serve a church that stifles your spirit. Our children will keep us tangled up in confusion. There are even times we find ourselves locked and loaded for nothing; a desolate land is our view, a wilderness for years and years—no lucrative destination in sight.

Man has the audacity to try and shut you down. They will minimize your psyche if allowed. They will hide your treasures. They will lie to you. They will steal from you. They will massacre your self-esteem and even your character; but you have given them the key — your key. You have given them power and dominion over you. You have allowed these minions to become gods in your life (Eze 14:3). *He* warns us that we should not worship any other god: for *He*, the *Lord God*, whose name is *Jealous*, *He* is a *jealous God*: **Jehovah Qanna** (Exod 34:14).

In all of these situations, there is a key that will unlock your very own personal prison — a key that will allow you to step out of the pit, a key that will welcome you into the palace, a key to the closet that houses your royal attire, a key to a spring of water that will satisfy your thirst (Isa 58:11). There's a cup running over with the eternal spring of water that will stir up the rivers of living water in your belly... that will justify your presence before the *King* of kings (John 7:38). The holy and true *Word*, *His* grace is sufficient (2 Cor 12:9); it empowers you to come boldly before the throne of grace (Heb 4:16). Prayer and petition, with thanksgiving to the living and true *God*, will unlock your treasures (Phil 4:6,7). Pray without ceasing (1 Thes 5:17).

He is the ***Redeemer***. *He* will recompense all that the adversary stole from you. *He* will correct every lie the enemy uttered to you and about you (Joel 2:25). *He* will destroy every stronghold that tried to deny you your rightful inheritance when you accept the keys from *Him* that is holy and true! Only *He* can unlock the treasures stored up for you. *He* has placed *His* signet on you and your destiny, giving you authority to have the *blessings* of *Abraham*. For all the promises of *God* in *Him* are 'yea', and in *Him* 'amen', unto the glory of *God* by us (2 Cor 1:20). *He* stands at the door knocking; if you hear *His* voice and use your key to open the door, *He* will come in, and you will share a meal together (Rev 3:20).

He that cometh to *God* must believe that *He* is, and that *He* is a rewarder of them that diligently seek *Him* (Heb 11:6). Take your key, acknowledge *Him* in all thy ways, seek *Him* for divine direction, follow *His* lead as *He* instructs you to the revelation of the mysteries and the treasures that *He* has ordained for you, and praise *Him* (Dan 2:22)! *He* tells you to call unto *Him*, and *He* will answer and tell you great and unsearchable things you do not know (Jer 33:3). Be encouraged to use your keys and walk in dominion and power for the glory of *Elohim*! *He* knows everything about you; when *He* looked upon *His* creation, *He* saw that it was very good (Gen 1:31).

#KINGDOMPEACES

Musings

What part of this 'Peace' stirred you and why?

_____
_____
_____
_____
_____
_____

Meanderings

Did this 'Peace' trigger any particular memory and why?

_____
_____
_____
_____
_____
_____
_____

Meditations

What secret place will you allow **Jehovah Rapha** to minister to you as you ponder this 'Peace'?

Knowing

Romans 8:28

Knowing... in the knowing... there is a knowing. Or simply 'just knowing.' Sounds deep... the deep places... crevices... crannies... cracks... in the structure. A place of no explanation — you just know. Some call it intuition. Some call it 'a feeling in my gut.' The rising of unexpected situations, that are tailgated with confusion, frustration piggy-backs as you search for an answer. A calm comes over you in such a peaceful manner that it takes a moment before you become cognizant of the change in the atmosphere (Isa 66:12). The tides have turned. That attack that felt so overwhelming has mellowed in its intensity, and you know that the battle has already been won (Luke 10:19). **Elohim**. **Creator**. Architect. Designer.

Our **Creator** designed us elaborately, and in **His** blueprint, **He** placed the 'knowing' within. That's why you can bask in confidence, knowing that **He** has already orchestrated your escape even before the attack began (1 Cor 10:13). **He** is **Alpha and Omega**! **He** stands in front of you and fights the battle, because the battle never belongs to you (1 Sam 17:47). **He** is **Jehovah Gibbor**, the *great* **God** that is mighty in battle (Psalm 24:8).

When evil is before you and it antagonizes you to no end, there's this innate urge to shun it — that's knowing (1 Thes 5:22). Just as Adam and Eve knew that the fruit was forbidden — the knowing prompted them to deny their flesh, but they denied the knowing (Gen 3:6,7).

When we defy the knowing in our lives, we find ourselves in many entanglements, seen and unseen. Understand that knowing is not of you. No, you're not that smart. No, you're not that wise. But we have this treasure in earthen vessels — that the excellency of the power may be of **God** and not of us (2 Cor 4:7). Long story short, it's not us. It's never us; it's always **Him**. Get in the 'know' and 'know' that **He** is all knowing because **He** is the knowing that shineth in you, **His** earthen vessel (Psa 139). Know that you know. There is not just a growing in the knowing; there is a glowing in the knowing.

Musings

What part of this 'Peace' stirred you and why?

_____
_____
_____
_____
_____
_____
_____

Meanderings

Did this 'Peace' trigger any particular memory and why?

_____
_____
_____
_____
_____
_____
_____

Meditations

What secret place will you allow **Jehovah Rapha** to minister to you as you ponder this 'Peace'?

Me Me Me

Psalm 27:8

I remember watching TV shows as a kid, and singers used this mantra as a tool to warm up their vocal cords. Modern day society has utilized these three simple words and aligned them under the platform deemed 'influencer.' The thirst for attention is addictive because the more likes you receive, the more you desire. Vanities of vanities; all vanity (Ecc 1:2). The increase of adoration builds up one's self-esteem, but should hold no value, because man is unstable in all his ways (James 1:8). The love that is poured on you in kindness and admiration can quickly turn to venom and treachery with an urgency designed to destroy. Like sand in an hourglass, the tables turn swiftly (Luke 6:26). Such is the heart of man, one moment pushing, prodding and promoting you; and in the blink of an eye, disappearing, and on to the next, the latest and the greatest (Mic 7:5). The abandonment of this liquid love leaves you scarred and dejected. What is man? But of the dust of the earth (Psa 103:14). That likened unto a flower that fadeth away to be remembered no more (Job 14:2).

The uphill journey is tedious but necessary, because once you conquer the trek, upon reflection you see the wonders that you passed along the way. People will come, people will go. Things that were of the utmost importance lose value with revelation (Matt 6:21). Purpose is only realized when the motive is deciphered. Once it is accomplished, or obtained, where is the happiness, the satisfaction? Happiness is temporary, but joy, that joy unspeakable, it is everlasting (Isa 51:11). The joy of the *Lord* is your strength (Neh 8:10)! Seek affirmation only from the *Everlasting God*! The *Eternal God* that calls you from faith to faith, strength to strength, and glory to glory. That *Everlasting Joy* in the palms of *His* holy hands; the place that *He* has designated just for you. Your name is engrafted in the palm of *His* hands (Rom 1:17; Psa 84:7; 2 Cor 3:18; Isa 49:16). As you look for the me in the me in the me, make sure you seek the *One* who knows the innermost parts of the 'me' and is able to renew your 'me' in *He* that is well able, above, beyond, exceeding your vivid imagination (Psa 94:22; Eph 3:20). Understand that the treasure you house in your earthen vessel is of the excellency of the power that be of the *Most High God*, and not of you (2 Cor 4:7).

Word to the wise: evacuate that empty, unfulfilled space of 'me' and delve into the innermost parts of *Him* that desires to fill you in

totality. Remember that *He* is not only a *just God*, a *righteous God*; *He* is also a *jealous God*, and *He* bids you not to be vain and practice idolatry (Exod 20:3-5). The elders speak of turning down your plate; be vigilant in turning away from the mirror seeking your reflection and be diligent in seeking *His* face, *His everlasting Word*, for that is what shall remain forever and ever (1 Pet 1:25). Let everything that has breath praise the *Lord* (Psa 150:6).

Musings

What part of this 'Peace' stirred you and why?

_____
_____
_____
_____
_____
_____

Meanderings

Did this 'Peace' trigger any particular memory and why?

_____
_____
_____
_____
_____
_____

Meditations

What secret place will you allow **Jehovah Rapha** to minister to you as you ponder this 'Peace'?

Measure

Ezekiel 47:1-12

Ezekiel was led by an angel of the **Most High** that was instructed to reveal a prophecy to him. He was at the river of healing. The angel showed him the flow of the water from different directions; then he led Ezekiel into the water as he was explaining the flow and the source. The angel began with a method of measuring the distance as they walked in the water. At one point, it was ankle deep. Upon measuring to walk further, it was knee deep. Later, it was waist deep. Once more, repeating the process, he went so far until a pivotal moment, seemingly a crossroad when walking was no longer an option and swimming would be required, the angel asked if he discerned the turn of motion.

The crossroad is a road many of us encounter. It's at this crucial juncture that we must make a decision. As we draw near to **Abba** and listen intentionally for **His** instruction, **He** will allow us to strategically only go so far, for the glory in relationship with **Yahweh** is knowing  that there is purpose in development in the attuning of the **Holy Spirit** that dwells within. **He** will never take you anywhere that will bring your destruction. **Jehovah Sabaoth** will always be your escape plan. As we seek **Him** in wisdom... in knowledge... in understanding... in revelation, we have to find refuge in believing that **He** knows the measure of man. **He** knows the design of our promises and propensity at all times.

Ezekiel was humble and obedient. He gave honor to

the vessel being used by the **Most High** and followed the leading of the **Holy Spirit**. Upon arrival back at the banks, the trees on the brink of the water were illuminated with clarity, and he was graced with the revelation of the grand purpose of trusting **God**, even in places that others would discount and overlook. **God** will provide (Gen 22:8). **He** is a great **God**; in some places in the Bible, it says **He** is terrible, which upon deeper inspection is interpreted as awesome (Psa 47:2). What an awesome **God** we serve!! Yes, **Lord**!

The angel gave Ezekiel divine revelation of all that the trees were purposed for. As **Yahweh** used the body of water that was deemed inoperative, **Yahweh** says, **I** will bless what **I** will bless and curse what **I** will curse (Gen 12:3). For **I Am** the beginning and end, **I** say what is good and what is bad. **I** can turn it all around for what the enemy intends for evil. **I, Yahweh** will use it for good! For **Elohim** is well able (Isa 5:20; Num 13:30)!

If Ezekiel had allowed his desires and thirst for more to distract him, he could have gotten himself in a mess — self-inflicted, of course. Ezekiel could have been disobedient and played into his curiosity and tried to extend the swim to delve further into the prophecy. The **Master** sets boundaries for each of us. Why? Because **He** knows what's best for us; how so? **He** told us that we are fearfully and wonderfully made, and our soul knows this very well.

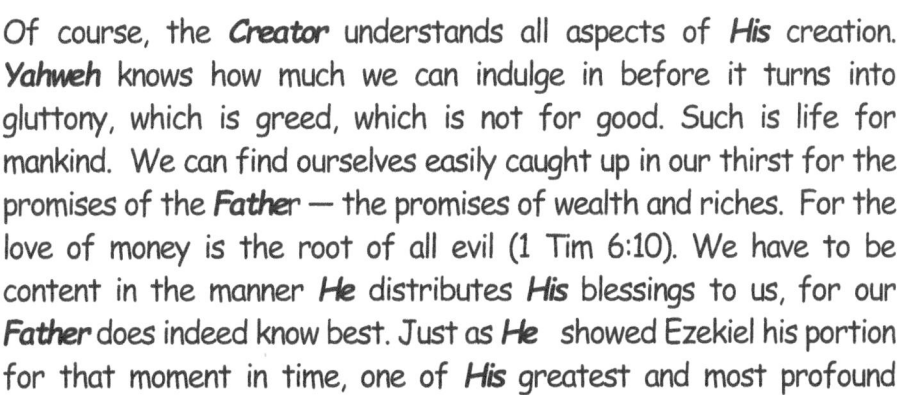

Of course, the **Creator** understands all aspects of **His** creation. **Yahweh** knows how much we can indulge in before it turns into gluttony, which is greed, which is not for good. Such is life for mankind. We can find ourselves easily caught up in our thirst for the promises of the **Father** — the promises of wealth and riches. For the love of money is the root of all evil (1 Tim 6:10). We have to be content in the manner **He** distributes **His** blessings to us, for our **Father** does indeed know best. Just as **He** showed Ezekiel his portion for that moment in time, one of **His** greatest and most profound

prophets. *Yahweh* kept *His* hand on Ezekiel for a greater purpose. Ezekiel honored *Yahweh* as his *Lord* and *Creator* and walked in obedience.

Yahweh wants us to seek *Him* diligently for direction. *He* instructs us to lean not to our own understanding, but to trust *Him* always (Pro 3:5,6). Like Ezekiel, if we heed *His* voice when we are led through waters, we won't become overwhelmed because *He* will bring us into safety. With obedience, wisdom, knowledge, and understanding comes the anointing of divine revelation (Isa 43:2). *He* will reveal the deep things at the proper time, for *He* knows *His* thoughts toward us, and *He* delivers just what we need at the appointed time (Dan 2:22).

He is so gracious that *He* removed the scales off of Ezekiel's eyes and anointed him with supernatural vision, knowledge, wisdom, and understanding. *He* opened his eyes to see that the greater was waiting on him. He didn't have to chase it; *Yahweh* had groomed Ezekiel for this experience. The angel explained the intricacies of what *Yahweh* was introducing him to: the trees not only provided meat and the leaf wouldn't die, but healing was within the leaves. The fish were in miraculous abundance. Ezekiel witnessed an extravagant overflow when he was led by the *Voice of God*.

Even when it appears as if others have the above, beyond, exceedingly and you're left to spectate, trust in *Him* for provision (Psa 49:16-18). *Jehovah Jirreh* knows, and *He* provides excessively to all those that trust in *Him* with all their hearts (Psa 9:10). *Abba Father* knows what's best for each of us — individually as well as collectively (Rom 12:3). *His* distribution is without reproach. *He* anointed giftings and callings to *His* people which are without repentance (Rom 11:29). *He* gave some to be apostles; and some, prophets; and some evangelists; and some, pastors and teachers for the perfecting of the saints (Eph 4:11). *He* knows exactly what *He* called each of us to do. Our task is to know *Him* intimately, so that when *He* calls us, we recognize *His* voice, and a stranger we will not follow (John 10:27)! **Elohim**, **Creator** of the heavens and the earth, and fullness thereof, knows all things — allow **Him** to be your measuring stick, for **He** makes no mistakes. **His** measuring stick is immeasurable.

Musings

What part of this 'Peace' stirred you and why?

_____
_____
_____
_____
_____
_____

Meanderings

Did this 'Peace' trigger any particular memory and why?

_____
_____
_____
_____
_____
_____
_____

Meditations

What secret place will you allow **Jehovah Rapha** to minister to you as you ponder this 'Peace'?

Miracles

Hebrews 2:4

Glory be to the **Most High**! Glory be to the *Father* of Lights (James 1:17)! Glory be to the *'shining star'* that illuminates a dark world. Glory be to the *infilling Spirit* of the *Holy One* as *He* impregnates *His* chosen vessels daily to birth new and amazing graces before an unbelieving world. We are Kingdom Changers — one small, magnificent miracle at a time.

He operates in miracles, signs, and wonders. A simple telephone call to encourage and check on someone's well-being may be the sign to that individual that **Abba Father** did indeed hear their prayer (Psa 66:19). Maybe it's in a shared conversation where there is an outpouring of edification among two believers that affirmation is received within the confirmation of the petition that was made in quiet meditation. *He* brought it to the forefront to confirm that *He* is ever-present. We exalt *Him* in *His* excellence for all of *His* ways are splendid (Psa 92:5)! Some are here today to testify that covid-19 did not take them out; while there are those who never had the virus. Both instances can attest that *El Roi* saw that the blood was on the doorpost, and there was indeed a *divine Passover*.

I ask that *You* continue to be a lamp to my feet and a light to my path as I travel this joyous journey in *You* (Psa 119:105). I find myself brimming and overflowing with peace and humility in the exaltation of *Your* presence, *Your* wisdom, and *Your* revelation! Hallelujah! Glory be to *Elohim*! *El Shaddai*... that knows my name, that knows the number of hairs on my head, that knows the inner workings of my mind, that knows the innermost desires of my heart, that cares about my flighty cares, that knows my destiny, and that loves me despite my sins and blots out all my transgressions (Luke 12:7; Jer 29:11; 1 John 1:9). Glory be to *Him* that cleanses me repeatedly upon request; for *He* is the source of my provision!

My *Spirit* leaps like a deer in a field with the fulfillment of *Your* presence that overshadows me and leaves seed for the sower and bread for the eater (Isa 55:10). All that I shall ever desire or need is in *Jehovah Jirreh*, and I worship *El Shaddai* from whom all my blessings flow (Gen 49:25-26). Hallelujah to *Jehovah Rapha* for the infusion of *His* healing virtue that filters my body continuously, and I diligently seek daily healing (Exod 15:26).

There is glory knowing that the weapons have formed; and my miracle is that they did not prosper because I stand on the foundation of the *Cornerstone* in which *His* church is built (Isa 28:16; 54:17)! As a chosen vessel, I bask in the revelation and understanding that a great work occurs daily in me. When I feel aches and pains, and I persevere despite the obstacles, and every time I call on the *Name* that is above every name, I witness the weapon of the adversary bowing down. Every time I arise from my sick bed, healed, I proclaim I am a miracle. I glory in my miracles when I pass an accident; it could have been me (Exod 12:13). I am constantly humbled when I read an obituary; I give *Him* praise because *His* grace and mercy blessed me with more chances — that is my miracle. When I walk across a parking lot, go shopping at the mall, make a 6-hour road trip, or go to work — things that shouldn't be taken for granted — I am grateful for each of my unmerited miracles.

I praise and worship *Him* for *His* abiding presence, for *His* power and *His* might, or, as I extol *Him*, for being the *Lily in the Valley*, because it's only in the valley of the shadow of death that I witness this unusual miracle. These are miraculous signs, and extraordinary wonders that have been prepared especially for me. It empowers me to sit at the table with my enemies and be kind, forgive, and be compassionate. It enables me to pray for those that misuse me knowing that *Jehovah Gibbor*, has already turned that word curse into a supernatural blessing, and I have to sit with them for them to witness *His* mighty graces upon me. Not because I'm so good, but that they see *Him* in me and know that a change has occurred. As they sip of the overflow out of my cup, their stony hearts may be turned, and they may experience the attuning of their hearts as *He* makes it flesh (Eze 36:26).

Thank *You* that nothing is wasted, even our time; that we miscount and crucify ourselves for what we call misused. The time that we spent talking to a friend, *You* used that communication, even if it felt unproductive, to allow *Your* presence to come forth because as believers it is our nature to speak of *You* somewhere in the conversation (Matt 18:20).

Thank *You*, *Holy Spirit*, for this ordained time to commune with *You*. For *You* love me implicitly, and I love *You* intentionally. It is with the utmost respect that I govern myself in this experience, and I recognize the richness of the intimacy between *You* and me. I acknowledge it counts for something because *You* are the nutrient in my life. *Your* voice is the heeding and leading of my life into the goodness and mercy of my *Shepherd* (Psa 23:1). Thank *You* for the fulfillment of the 'yes' and the 'Amen' in *Him* that loves me unconditionally, and *His* unblemished blood provides me with abundant and everlasting love (2 Cor 1:20). Thank *You* for ushering me into *His* gates with thanksgiving and into *His* courts with praises, truly understanding the revelation of the honor and the privilege, of glorifying *Him* as *Almighty* (Psa 100:4). Thank *You*, *Holy Spirit*, for opportunities to go to the altar and bow at *His* feet and just worship *Him* in honesty. Unhindered worship of *Him* for being great and mighty, loving and kind, for being *King* of kings, for being *Lord* of lords, for being the all in all, for allowing a wretch like me to be called *His Beloved*. Thank *You*, *Holy Spirit*! Thank *You Jesus*, for the gift of the *Holy Spirit*! Thank *You*, *Father God*, for *Jesus*, the *Savior* of the world, the *Messiah*, the *slain Lamb of God*! Thank *You*, *Abba Father*, for being such a good *Father*, for being-*El Emuwnah*! Thank *You*, *Abba Father*, for the engrafting of me into this divine family of unfathomable love! Thank *You* for the miracle that is me in *You*! Thank *You* for creating me as one of *Your* divine miracles! I am a miracle! Hallelujah! Amen! It Is So!

Musings

What part of this 'Peace' stirred you and why?

_____
_____
_____
_____
_____
_____

Meanderings

Did this 'Peace' trigger any particular memory and why?

_____
_____
_____
_____
_____
_____
_____

Meditations

What secret place will you allow **Jehovah Rapha** to minister to you as you ponder this 'Peace'?

Never

Psalm 37:25

Remember those times that it seemed as if all the cards were stacked against you. When the way was so murky that the heaviness of it all seemed to consume and overwhelm you. That which was seen was without hope and you felt hopeless, betrayed and alone (Rom 8:24). Yeah, those days. Days that are behind you, praise **El Shaddai**. Days that seemed never-ending. Days that seemed like weeks, months, and years for some of us. In the peripheral eye, your imagination could depict you as a truck stuck in a muddy rut, and the more you attempted to change gear and bully your way through, the deeper the hole seemed. Days that tears put you to sleep and woke you up with even more patterns of despair (Psa 6:6). Those were times you felt like Lyfe Jennings, as he spoke of looking under the couch, under the bed, and in the closets for the **Master** to stand up and fight the battles. During those times, it seems the more places you looked, the deeper your troubles; they seem to be illuminated with a blinding glare for all to witness (Psa 25:17). Now it seems as if all eyes are on you... and if their eyes are on you, you know their mouths are going 90 to nothing... then you envision you are fodder for the day.

Gloom and doom have but a brief respite before it has to move on. Motivational speaker, Tommie Harris once said "That cloud can't stay in one place, it has to move." Believe that. Have you ever taken the time to just watch the constant motion of the clouds in the heavens and reflect on your

life composition? Because as you were searching for the *Master*. *He* always knew where you were. Remember, *He* is all-knowing. While you were in that hole, *He* was ministering to the spirit of heaviness that was weighing you down. No matter how deep the hole you wallowed in, *He* was omnipresent, and because of *His* presence, you have the joy of 'looking back'… right (Josh 1:9)? That place of hopelessness — you're no longer there. Whether you gained a mile, a few feet, or even an inch; you moved by the *grace of God*.

Jehovah Rohi will never allow you to go anywhere that *He* won't deliver you (1 Corinthians 10:13). *He* is your deliverer from dangers seen and unseen, known and unknown, deserved or undeserved (Psa 103:10). Even if an army surrounds you — and war rises against you — when the *Lord* is your light and your salvation, who shall you fear (Psa 27:3, 1)? CeCe Winans sings lyrically of *Jesus* never losing a battle. For the *Lord* your *God* goes with you; *He* will fight your enemies and give you a sure victory (Deut 20:4). For the weapons of our warfare are not worldly, but mighty through *God* to the pulling down of strongholds (2 Cor 4:10).

Though trouble may be on every side, on each corner, and in all directions, though, you find yourself perplexed, confused about the onslaught of tribulations, even though you may be persecuted with injustices you never thought imaginable… My *Lord*! When you are struck down… be not distressed… give despair no glory… look to *Jehovah Shammah*… and stand firm, be resolved knowing that *Yahweh*, the *Great I Am*, has never lost a battle… *He* has never conceded to anyone or anything, for *He* is *Elohim*… that which is created was created by *Him*, for *Him*, and with *Him* (2 Cor 4:8; John 1:3).

He has a purpose for all *He* allows. Whether you are on the potter's wheel or going through the purifying fire, or even being dipped in healing waters, nothing is wasted (2 Timothy 1:9).

Jehovah Nissi is so powerful! ***He*** is so mighty! It does not matter what comes against you; evil shall not overcome good (Rom 12:21). Though they plot evil against you and devise wicked schemes, they cannot succeed (Psa 21:11). Because ***He*** is ***Jehovah Gibbor***, the ***Lord God mighty in battle*** and ***He*** shall always be victorious! There has never been a battle lost in ***Jesus Christ***, the unblemished ***Lamb of God***. Everyone born of ***God*** overcomes the world, and this is the victory in ***Christ*** (1 John 5:4). I've been young, and now I am old, but I've never seen the righteous forsaken nor its seed begging bread (Psa 37:25). We as heirs of ***God***, joint-heirs in ***Christ***, don't have to beg ***Abba Father***. For if a good father, in all his flaws, will do all he can for his children, how much more our ***Father*** which art in heaven (Rom 8:17,15; Matt 7:11). Find joy in all situations, knowing that the trying of your faith produces patience which works for the good of those who love the ***Lord*** and are called according to ***His*** purpose (James 1:3; Rom 8:28). Nothing is wasted, and never has ***He*** lost a battle.

Musings

What part of this 'Peace' stirred you and why?

_____
_____
_____
_____
_____
_____

Meanderings

Did this 'Peace' trigger any particular memory and why?

_____
_____
_____
_____
_____
_____
_____

Meditations

What secret place will you allow **Jehovah Rapha** to minister to you as you ponder this 'Peace'?

Out With the Old

2 Corinthians 5:17

New beginnings are exciting, especially when they have been long awaited. They are fresh, but can also be intimidating. We hate to mar our blessings with that vapid word, fear — we plead the *blood of Jesus* over that spirit of bondage. Spring cleaning motivates you to clean out your closets and get rid of clothes that you've held on to for five years waiting for those distressful 25 pounds to melt away from you. For the 15 new outfits, you get rid of 8 old ones. It still doesn't seem like an even swap; the good still outweighs the bad (Rom 14:16). That's how *God* operates — no matter how big the sacrifice may seem to us; it's diminutive to *El Shaddai* (Heb 10:14).

When people are blessed with a new house, most don't want to take their old furniture into the new house; the homeowner embraces the 'newness' in their lives (2 Cor 5:17). Not to say that there is anything wrong with either option, but that's how we should perceive our lives. When we accept *Jesus Christ* as our *Savior* for real, and for true — when we've gotten weary of having a fleeting affair with the *lover of our soul*... when we finally surrender all unto *Him* — we want our house to be cleansed from the old garbage (Jer 31:3). We desire for *Elohim* to remove that stony heart that had waxed cold and that wicked spirit that chased evil; we seek *Him* for a new heart, and a new spirit, and the

heart of flesh (Matt 24:12; Eze 36:26). We desire to yield to the newness and purity of the *Godly* spirit and heart. We no longer crave those activities that we used to do, those misdeeds (2 Cor 5:17).

When you close the portals to the old, the evil and the undesirables that left you empty and unfulfilled, there is a glory that will manifest over your new endeavors. Your lifestyle (mind) will be renewed once you establish that you've pushed past the old (Rom 12:2). That you pursue the peace of the new things discovered within the promises of *Father*, the 'yea', and the 'Amen' in *Jesus* (Psa 34:14; 2 Cor 1:20). The gift that lives with the life of a blood-washed believer. That no matter what comes, because evil will still war with your flesh for your soul, you have nothing left of the old man; he was evicted and has been served notice, and he will not be welcomed back in (Prov 20:8). There is a new landlord in your establishment. **He's *Alpha*** and ***Omega***, the entrance and the exit, and *He* declared your new house a temple of the *Holy Ghost* (1 Cor 3:16). This house has been bought with a price, and it will not be sold anymore (1 Cor 6:19). You are healed, sealed and delivered... you are souled out! In *Jesus* Name! Amen!

Musings

What part of this 'Peace' stirred you and why?

_____
_____
_____
_____
_____
_____
_____

Meanderings

Did this 'Peace' trigger any particular memory and why?

_____
_____
_____
_____
_____
_____
_____

Meditations

What secret place will you allow **Jehovah Rapha** to minister to you as you ponder this 'Peace'?

_____
_____
_____
_____
_____
_____
_____
_____
_____
_____
_____
_____
_____
_____
_____
_____

Pick

Matthew 22:14

Have you ever had your heart broken because you were not picked? Have you ever had your dreams assassinated after you did everything right, perfected everything, and still you found yourself in the reject pile? Have you ever been disillusioned by a system that promoted one thing, yet did something entirely different?

Year after year, the NBA creates a humongous fanfare with the projection of draft picks — building the bidding and betting based on images with statistics and history to validate their candidates — and in the end, someone is left standing at the door of opportunity as it closes on their hopes and dreams. That's a grandstand scenario; what about when it's within the family?

What about when you are always the one who has to stand in the gap, yet when it's time to choose, you are the forgotten one? Not one time, not two times, but every time, which leaves you frustrated. Who does that? Where and why does that happen? How can this even be a reality? Who wrote this story? Make it make sense!

When you choose the right over the wrong; when you choose to stand instead of sit, run instead of walk, or when you choose to tell the truth and shame the devil; yet, you are never the 'pick.' The method to this meticulous madness has an algorithm that's indescribable — and it seems to never work in your favor. Overlooked, misunderstood,

and mistreated becomes your new mantra.

Rejection is never desirable. It's an appearance that is not comely and seems to serve no purpose that's worth speaking of. It tears down your self-esteem. It destroys your ability to hope, and it interchanges your dreams and manifests them into morbid nightmares. All because you seem to never be 'picked' for anything.

In these misalignments with people, being with the wrong crowd, hanging out in the wrong places, acknowledge that maybe you are making some bad choices. Perhaps you are 'picking' the wrong things that will only satisfy the lust of the eye.

We've mulled over all the dismal realities. Let's take a bird's-eye view and see what happens when you are ripe for the 'picking.' Forgetting about those things that are behind you, (Phil 3:13) reaching for better things and praying that better days are coming for you.

There is one that awaits your arrival. *He* waits for you to be open to receive the revelation that *He* picked you. *He* chose you — you did not choose *Him* (Eph 1:4). *He* not only picked you, but *He* ordained you to go out and bear fruit, and to be a *Kingdom Builder* (John 15:16). The **Resurrected Christ** picked you long before you even knew *Him*. *He* knew all about you. *He* knew that there would be a day when you would grow weary in placing all of your hopes in the hands of someone who doesn't have your best interests at heart.

Your hope was in the temporal, the corruptible accolades and things of the world. The desire to be picked by your peers for superficial opportunities that will wither like flowers. We work for trophies and medals that will decay, that come to nothing, and remembered no more (Matt 6:19). Athletes train and discipline themselves as they prepare to compete in games; their aspiration is for a crown of victory, of completion; yet the greatest accomplishment is in **Jesus Christ**, in which the winner receives an imperishable crown (1 Cor

9:25). *Jesus* knows your heart. *He* knows your deepest desires. *He* knows the depth of your soul. *He* knows the infinite design of you — potentials and blatant flaws (Luke 16:15). And in spite of the failures; *He* always picks you. *His* team is eternal, from everlasting to everlasting.

God foreknew King David; even though David was a musty shepherd boy; the brother that no one paid any attention to, he was an afterthought, even to Jesse, his father. Even when everyone overlooked David, he remained devoted to his task; he was a great shepherd. David knew that as he was overlooked, sheep could be overlooked as well, so he was diligent in tending to them, because he knew they possessed great potential for gain for his family. David understood that to be a great leader, you have to be an even greater servant.

God was grooming him in humility and steadfastness. When *God* sent Samuel to Jesse to anoint the next king, *He* already knew the playbook. Yet, as always, *He* allowed man to prolong the obvious, and only after Jesse had exhausted all efforts was *God's* ordination fulfilled. David wasn't the first pick; he was the last pick (1 Sam 16). The first shall be last, and the last shall be first: for many are called; but few are chosen (Matt 20:16).

David is a prime example in understanding that there is sometimes a season of waiting. Sometimes you may have to endure a season of rejection, a season of uncertainty and denial. But there is *One* that will fight for you and allow you to hold your peace (Exod 14:14). *He* promised that *He* would give you the desires of your heart if you would seek *Him*, *He* would be found by you (1 Chr 28:9).

I implore you to stop worrying; leave the pity party on the curb, trust in the *Master Orchestrator*, the *Greatest Narrator*, the *Grandest Orator*, the *Ultimate Writer*, Producer and Director; **Elohim**.

#KINGDOMPEACES

Musings

What part of this 'Peace' stirred you and why?

_____
_____
_____
_____
_____
_____
_____

Meanderings

Did this 'Peace' trigger any particular memory and why?

_____
_____
_____
_____
_____
_____
_____

Meditations

What secret place will you allow **Jehovah Rapha** to minister to you as you ponder this 'Peace'?

Prosper

3 John 1:2

Prosper... prosperity... success... abundance... overflow... all these words bring a genuine smile to your face. The flesh lusts after prosperity and all of its many benefits. It would seem to evoke grace, the effervescence of all that is good. When we look toward the hope for prosperity, we think we can work our way out of a place of lack, a position of poverty, a place that should not be comfortable in most people's opinion. The world spouts of the goodness in prospering. The world tells us we should all be striving for more, more and even more. We want to prosper with more money, which calls for the prospering of more time; which calls for the prospering of more energy, which calls for the prospering of more of you. Sometimes in the busyness of prospering, you lose your most precious gift, the prosperity of self. You find yourself in a place of despondency, confusion, disillusionment, and vacancy. The storehouse may run over with the prosperity of the world; but there is a vital deficiency of that place called peace. Peace of mind is priceless. Prosperity can never afford you peace when it's of self.

What is it to gain the world and lose your soul (Mark 8:36)? *God* said that *He* would supply all of our needs according to *His* riches in glory (Phil 4:19). Obedience is better than sacrifice; oh, the many sacrifices we make to honor man and the world for the art of prospering (1 Sam 15:22). Even when we know that the love of

money is the root of all evil, we still will chase after it (1 Tim 6:10). What would the world look like if man chased after the **King** of kings with the same fervency as we do for the worldly riches that fadeth away (1 John 2:17)? **God** said that **He** giveth thee power to get wealth, that a covenant might be established (Deut 8:18). **He** told us that wealth and riches shall be in the house of those that fear **Him** (Psa 112:3). The **Father** has blessed us with all spiritual blessings in heavenly places in **Christ Jesus** (Eph 1:3). Oh, but if we would receive the revelation, we would indeed stand under an open heaven. The joy of the **Lord** would be our strength (Neh 8:10). That's the prosperity that our souls yearn for. Our souls will find true satisfaction when we understand that our inheritance is predestinated. Our **Father** would have it that we would prosper in all areas of our lives; that we would not just prosper in wealth, but in health as our soul prospers (3 John 1:2). Our **Father** is generous. **He** doesn't want there to be any lack — only overflow. Our inheritance is in **Christ,** who paid the price that we might indeed prosper in **Him** from whom all blessings flow. The blessing of the **Lord**, it maketh rich and adds no sorrow (Prov 10:22). I encourage you to find your prospering in our **Lord** and **Savior** for in **Him** lies eternal wealth. **Jehovah Chayil, God** of Wealth. The everlasting wealthy place. May you thrive in the prosperity of the gift of the **Messiah.**

Musings

What part of this 'Peace' stirred you and why?

_____
_____
_____
_____
_____
_____
_____

Meanderings

Did this 'Peace' trigger any particular memory and why?

_____
_____
_____
_____
_____
_____
_____

Meditations

What secret place will you allow **Jehovah Rapha** to minister to you as you ponder this 'Peace'?

Pusher

1 John 4:1

In the 1970s, there was a song that shamelessly boasted, "I'm your pusher man." The reference was to a drug dealer claiming his title and his job in delivering destruction to humankind. This pusher delivered mass devastation as he stole, killed, and destroyed families — stealing husbands from wives; mothers  from children, totally obliterated families. His actions annihilated dignity and integrity and promoted places of desolation, places of no morals or standards. A place of hopelessness.

In most cities, there is a church on every corner, and the majority of them push the *Word of **God***. The quickening *Word of the **Most High***. The *Word* that brings down the high tree, dries up the green tree, but also has the ability to exalt the low tree, and cause the same dry tree to flourish (Eze 17:24). The *Word* that will whisper your prayers of covering in the ear of the prodigal son or daughter as they shun their calling. The *Word* that heals the sick. The *Word* that opens the eyes of the blind, triggers the hearing of the deaf, opens the mouth of the mute, and calls for the dead to be resurrected by the *Spirit of the living and true **God*** (Jer 30:17). ***Elohim*** is patient with you, not wanting anyone to perish, but that everyone come to repentance (2 Pet 3:9). How so? How can one hear without a preacher (Rom 10:14)? ***He Himself*** gave some to be apostles, some prophets, some evangelists, and some pastors and teachers, for the equipping of the saints for the edifying of the body of **Christ** (Eph 4:11). As Abraham said, "My **God** will provide, for **He** is indeed **Jehovah Jirreh**" (Gen 22:8). **He** supplies every need according to **His** endless riches in glory (Phil 4:19).

In life there will be places we will need to be pushed, but we have a choice to which path we choose. The path to live in squalor, in sin, in lack and insufficiency — for it is broad; it is wide — it is comfortable because it is easy. There is no motivation to live better — maybe to live bitter; maybe to indulge in the lusts of the flesh which will never be satisfied or quenched, but it will always strive for even more desecration, as it drains you of every vestige of power you wield.

Hold up! There is a place of rejuvenation... regeneration... restoration... restitution... and it is in the **Resurrected Christ**. **He's** so mild and meek that **He** doesn't push **Himself** or **His** goodness on you. **He** doesn't charge an astronomical fee for what will bless you beyond measure (Matt 11:28-20). **He** gives you the gift upon acceptance of **Him** as your **Savior**. The gift that keeps on giving; the **Comforter**, the **Holy Spirit** will give you an unction that propels you, that pushes you toward the mark for the prize of the high calling of **God** in **Christ Jesus** (1 John 2:20; Phil 3:14).

Yes, in life there will be innumerable encounters with various pushers. Some are assigned to promote you... some are assigned to demote you. Your responsibility is to ask the **Holy Spirit** to guide you so that you don't allow that destructive pusher to push you over the edge of the cliff from which there is no return. Your pusher should be anointed by the *living and true God* and yield intentions of uplifting being that you will naturally as well as spiritually witness the manifestation of yourself ascending to higher heights designated for you in **Christ** (1 Thes 5:11).

The presence of **God** in this pusher will overshadow all fear and trepidation as you walk in the revelation of power, of love and of a sound mind (2 Tim 1:7). Always seek *Jesus Christ* as your pusher man, for in **Christ** there is no failure. **He** came that you might have life and life in abundance (John 10:10). Seek ye first the *kingdom of God*, and all these things will be added unto you (Matt 6:33). *Jesus Christ* is the fullness of the all-in-all. Rest in the blessed assurance of the pusher that is intentional in your prospering, your future and your hope! *Jesus*!

#KINGDOMPEACES

Musings

What part of this 'Peace' stirred you and why?

_____
_____
_____
_____
_____
_____

Meanderings

Did this 'Peace' trigger any particular memory and why?

_____
_____
_____
_____
_____
_____
_____

Meditations

What secret place will you allow **Jehovah Rapha** to minister to you as you ponder this 'Peace'?

_____
_____
_____
_____
_____
_____
_____
_____
_____
_____
_____
_____
_____
_____
_____

Rain

Zechariah 10:1

It's gonna rain! It's gonna rain! When it rains, what will you be doing (Isa 10:3)? Will you run and hide in fear, or will you race toward the rain with holy hands lifted unto heaven? *El Roi* sees; *El Roi* not only sees, but *He* knows everything (Gen 16:13). *He* knows the seasons of harvest. *He* knows the seasons of drought. *He* knows the time and times and the dividing of times (Dan 7:21). *He* knows when we need to sit in our works, in our acts, in our emotions, in our rebellious states — *He* knows. *He* knows when we need to be rescued from the miry clay, when we need to see *Him* extend *His* righteous right hand, when we need to see *Him* avenge our injustices, when we need to just be in our stillness, and know that *He* is *God* (Luke 18:8; Psa 46:10).

How can two walk together unless they agree (Amos 3:3)? Two may sow unrighteous seed together, but may not reap it together; for to each there is a day of reckoning, no matter the offense. We may sow seeds of righteousness corporately to the glory of the *living and the true God*, but our reward may not be reaped in the same measure or even in the same season. Who can measure the *grace of God*? But every one of us is given grace according to the measure of the gift of *Christ* (Eph 4:7). As children of the *Most High God*, we know that *He* maketh *His* sun to rise on the evil and on the good, and sendeth rain on the just and on the unjust (Matt 5:45).

Who is like our *merciful God*, who pardons our sins among *His* people (Isa 43:25)? Our *God* that will not remain angry because *He* delights in mercy and lovingkindness (Mic 7:18). *His* anger is, but for a moment; in *His* favor is life (Psa 30:5).

Many times, in life we like Job question **God** about the falling of rain in our lives. Sometimes there's a downpour that blinds us. It's raining so hard that we can't see, and we cannot discern; we are not even able to decipher direction, less known instruction. It's in these typhoon-like rainfalls that we understand the disciples' fear in the boat when the storm arose and tossed them to and fro, and yet **Jesus** slept unbothered (Matt 8:23-27). It's only in these types of storms that we come to the divine revelation that **Jesus Christ** is the *captain of our Salvation* (Heb 2:10). More often than not, it's in these harsh circumstances that have been activated to immeasurable heights that we too, like the disciples, cry out to **Jesus** and ask **Him** if **He** cares that we perish (Mark 4:38)? We too, like the martyrs, may cry unto **God**, asking **Him** how long before **He** judges and avenges (Rev 6:10). We too, seek **Jesus** for three simple yet powerful and poignant words.

Peace. Be. Still (Mark 4:39). We must believe before we are open to receive **His** righteous rain of redemption, of restoration, of revival, of refreshment in this purpose-driven rain. We relish the release of the latter rain as it cleanses us of all unrighteousness and turns the tide of wretchedness to righteousness. Retribution comes with the latter rain, for its refreshening, knowing that **He** does care (Zech 10:1). Our desires change; we no longer seek to perform in the reign of a kingdom of evil and malice; but we thirst for the *living water* which quenches and fulfills (John 4:14). It is then, that we wholeheartedly rush into the rain from heaven that man has no control or authority to disburse (Joel 2:23).

Let it rain, **Father God**, let it rain! Let **Your** glory rain on us that we might feel **Your** abiding presence. Let us, like the earth, drink in the rain. Allow us, like the earth, to bring forth the fruits for which **You** have groomed us to produce. Let us, like the earth, receive the blessings of **El Shaddai** (John 15:16; Rom 7:4).

Father, we don't want to be like thorns and thistles that **You** reject and receive **Your** wrath; that will only receive curses, that will be burned (Heb 6:8). We have no desire to be fearful when we hear the rain. Let us acknowledge **You** as the *just **God***, knowing that **You** are our avenger (2 Thes 1:6-8). Let us receive the rain as we call upon **You** as **Jehovah M'Kaddesh**, for we have been sanctified to receive this rain from **You**, **Jehovah Rohi**, our **Great Shepherd**. Thank **You** for sending our **Savior**, that we have been redeemed from the curse of death and restored to receive the rain of eternal life (Gal 3:13). Thank **You** for the rain. We will be mindful to give **You** all the glory! For **You, Father God**, are honor! **You, Father God**, are glory! **You, Father God**, are praise!!!

Let it rain! Let it rain! May **You** open up the windows of heaven, and pour out **Your** blessing that there shall not be room enough to receive it (Mal 4:10)! Let **Your** rain be upon us as righteousness. **Jehovah Tsidkenu**! Let it rain!

Musings

What part of this 'Peace' stirred you and why?

_____
_____
_____
_____
_____
_____

Meanderings

Did this 'Peace' trigger any particular memory and why?

_____
_____
_____
_____
_____
_____
_____

Meditations

What secret place will you allow **Jehovah Rapha** to minister to you as you ponder this 'Peace'?

Reminder

Hebrews 6:10

The fullness of life includes people, places, and things. The fullness of life entails many events and instances that your presence is not only needed, but it is a prerequisite. The need for you is fulfilling in most circumstances, yet can be overwhelming with the influx of time and times and the dividing of times (Dan 7:25).

Many seek organization in the confidence that they don't forget or miss an assignment, and in this fast-paced life, we all need reminders. Some people have planners, some use notebooks, and some cleverly utilize the app on their smartphones to aid them in staying attuned to their numerous tasks. So many places to go, so many people to see, so many things to do. What is a mere 24 hours? How do you prioritize these many responsibilities that accost you on a daily basis? Reminders, I must be reminded to remember.

Yet, there is a reminder that works not for your good; he is adversarial; he is controversial; he is the prosecuting attorney that keeps account of all your illegal offenses (Psa 109:6). He not only bears witness, but he retains records to be presented against you in the courts of heaven (Zech 3:1). This reminder is the 'accuser' — the infamous and tireless one that because of his fallen state in creation, thrives in the destruction (desecration) of **God's** greatest creation, man (Rev 12:10). He lives to torment you because he has a tormented soul with a destiny that speaks of

engulfing fire, brimstone and destruction that will be for eternity (Rev 20:10). His legacy is built on being oppositional and destroying the *kingdom of God*. While perusing your life and the life of those attached to you, even the lives of strangers that somehow you are privy to their story, you notate the constant and consistent presence of the devourer as he is intentional in theft, murder and massacre — patterns of devastation (John 10:10).

But believers of the **Resurrected Christ** can find an extraordinary joy that there is a great 'Reminder' that we find comfort in — the gift that **Jesus Christ** left for **His** followers before **He** ascended to **His** rightful place of authority of dominion at the right hand of the **Father** (Acts 1:9; 2:1-4; 7:56). The **Father** sent this 'Reminder' in the name of the **Resurrected Christ**, that we should be taught all things, and that this 'Reminder' would bring to our remembrance all things, all that the **Father** had said to us and about us (John 14:26). Our beloved 'Reminder' strengthens our faith by consistently keeping us abreast of the devices of the devious enemy (2 Cor 2:11). This 'Reminder' affirms our dominion in the land as we are reminded that we are created in **Elohim's** image... that we are fearfully and wonderfully made... that we are of **His** marvelous works (Gen 1:26; Psa 139:14). This 'Reminder' brings to remembrance that many are the afflictions of the righteous; but the **Lord** delivers him of them all (Psa 34:19).

Be strong and of good courage. Do not fear nor be afraid of what the accuser speaks against you; for the **Lord**, your **God**, **He** is the one who goes with you. **He** will not leave you nor forsake you (Deut 31:6, 8). Do not fear nor be dismayed, for it is the **Lord** who goes before you — the *slain* **Lamb of God**, for **He** reigns victorious, **He** reigns faithful, **He** reigns truth, **He** reigns justice, and **He** reigns eternal (Rev 5:6-10)!

It's advantageous for believers to keep one another encouraged while witnessing *His* power, *His* might, and *His* grace with reverential fear, being mindful to give only *Him* all the glory and all the praise (Dan 4:34)! These have been written in **Elohim's** Book of Remembrance (Mal 3:16). Allow eternal joy to be your strength in the **Lord** (Neh 8:10). Men will forget, but our peace is in the guarantee that **God** remembers. *He* is faithful when we are faithless (2 Tim 2:13). Not only does **God** remember—*He* supplies (**Jehovah Jireh**) as a *Reminder*.' Take solace no matter what challenges you must endure because as believers of the **Resurrected Christ**, we serve *the living and the true God;* our salvation has been secured by the *blood of the slain Lamb of God*, and we have been gifted with the *indwelling Spirit* who serves us in innumerable ways but also as a *'Reminder'* (Rev 12:11). Glory be to the **Most High** for *He* is greatly to be praised!

Musings

What part of this 'Peace' stirred you and why?

_____
_____
_____
_____
_____
_____

Meanderings

Did this 'Peace' trigger any particular memory and why?

_____
_____
_____
_____
_____
_____

Meditations

What secret place will you allow **Jehovah Rapha** to minister to you as you ponder this 'Peace'?

Season Vs Lifestyle

Ecclesiastes 3

The **Father** tells us there are different seasons in our lives. There's a time to rejoice and a time to mourn. There's a time to seek and a time to sit. There's a time to speak emphatically, and there is a time to marinate gracefully. For everything under the sun, there is a season (Ecc 3).

Man, that is born of a woman is of a few days, and full of trouble (Job 14:1). There will be some glorious days, and there will be some gloomy days; each day has its portion, and man can eat and leave or choose to become gluttonous with their indulgences and become stagnant in that situation. Just as King David mourned the loss of his child with Bathsheba, he cried out to **God** for mercy; but once the **Lord** had spoken, King David trusted in the **Lord**. He removed his grave clothes and chose to live. King David believed in the goodness of the **Lord**, and that the **Most High** was all-knowing. **He** accepted the season (2 Sam 12:15-23).

For some the season may be days; some weeks, some months, and for some years, but to each its own. This is personal, and each one has to seek **God** in their season of sorrow, pulling on the hem of **His** garment, calling on **Him** to heal their broken hearts, to bind up their wounds, believing that **He** will do just what we ask (Psa 147:3). There will come a time when choices have to be made: a season or a lifestyle.

The loss of a loved one can be hurtful, even when we know that death is welcomed by the one who is suffering indescribably. So, what about the unexpected death — the leaving of our loved one without warning, the loved one's death that has taken us by surprise; the residue of their transition leaving the loved ones in a tomb of devastation?

Broken hearts allow the tears free rein. Life becomes a fog as you may find yourself functioning on auto-pilot, all while your mind is consumed with grief. Fear creeps in and overshadows you. You discover the fear to live and the fear to die grips your mentality as you attempt to decipher what *God's* purpose is in the giving and the taking (Job 1:21). Trying to scramble up the faith to say 'blessed be the name of the *Lord* (Dan 2:20). The inner you knows that *He* is good, but the flesh — oh, that battle is real, and you feel each internally love-inflicted scar from the warfare with the flesh.

God made a promise, and *He* is a *Covenant-Keeping God*. *He* is a *Promise-Keeper!* *He* promised *His* heirs that *He* would never leave them nor forsake them (Deut 31:6). *He* promised that neither life nor death could separate us from *His* love (Rom 8:38). *Elohim* is the only one that can make that promise and keep it (Rev 22:13). *He* is the giver of life, from the moment *He* blew breath in Adam, and the taker, when *He* will receive the saint's spirit unto *Himself* (Job 34:14,15). The *Lord* gives, and the *Lord* takes away, blessed be the name of the *Lord* (Job 1:21).

He instructs us to *not* cry as if we have no hope, for *He* is our *Hope of Glory* (1 Thes 4:13-18; Col 1:27). *Jesus Christ* came that we might live life abundantly (John 10:10). The anointing of *Jesus Christ* was fulfilled when *He* obtained the keys to death and hell (Rev 1:18). *He* took the sting of death away, so that there would be peace in the valley of the shadow of death, not fear (1 Cor 15:55; Psa 23:4). Choose *Him* who gave *His* life willingly that you might live in liberty to follow in *His*

footsteps doing good works (Titus 2:14). Live an abundant life daily, knowing that *He* paid for it all (Psa 118:24). Remember, weeping may endure for a night, but joy comes in the morning (Psa 30:5). It is a season... not a lifestyle.

Musings

What part of this 'Peace' stirred you and why?

_____
_____
_____
_____
_____
_____

Meanderings

Did this 'Peace' trigger any particular memory and why?

_____
_____
_____
_____
_____
_____
_____

Meditations

What secret place will you allow **Jehovah Rapha** to minister to you as you ponder this 'Peace'?

_____
_____
_____
_____
_____
_____
_____
_____
_____
_____
_____
_____
_____
_____
_____
_____

Seekers

Matthew 6:33

Today's society beckons us to desire more and more of so many things. Advertisements entice with the promise of weight loss, wrinkle-free skin, beautiful hair, flawless bodies, perfect credit, established careers. All come with a contingency of reciprocity. The promises of greater, better, grander — all things that make you go *Mmmm*, because it would satisfy or quench that place that hungers and thirsts for more, and you seek to fulfill.

Many times, we invest too heavily into the façade(s) that is/are presented of perfection all the while maintaining the mindset of accepting 75% of it coming into fruition. Disbelief. Disbelief hinders us from believing that 100% is possible. Why? Because after chasing so many perfectly painted portraits and always discovering cracks in the structure, the visions become marred with disillusionment in believing that 'anything is possible' (1 John 2:15-17).

Yet there is a treasure trove that is open to all. It was with you at the beginning and will be with you in the marked end. There is no limitation on the amount that you can ingest, and even a perceived excessive amount will not be considered gluttonous. The secret treasure, this hidden treasure, is in plain sight of everyone. It is the *Word of **God***. In the beginning was the ***Word***, and the ***Word*** was with ***God***, and the ***Word*** was ***God*** (John 1:1). Every encounter that you experience, every landscape that you identify, every piece of rough terrain that you excavate, every mountain that you scale has been overcome before you perceive it (John 16:33).

Jesus instructed us not to worry about or ponder the inconsequential frivolousness of the world. *He* specifically said, "Seek ye first the *Kingdom of God* and *His* righteousness, and all these things will be added to you (Matt 6:33)." The prophet Jeremiah relayed the message that **Abba Father** said: when you seek *Him* with your whole heart, you will find *Him* (Jer 29:13).

He's not looking for a 75/25; *He* desires the heart of man being in pursuit of *Him*, not happiness, not wealth nor riches of this world, not titles nor status, not reputation nor accreditation, but *Him*. *Yahweh*. The *I Am* that *I Am* (Exod 3:14). *He* makes provision for *His* children. *His* desire is to bless *His* children, for *He* is an amazing *God*; the one living and true *God* who is all wise, all knowing and almighty. *His* desire is for the land to be blessed. *His* desire is for *His* people to be blessed (Isa 58:11). *His* desire is for healing to radiate the earth as far as the north is from the south, and the east from the west. *His* desire is for *His* people who recognize *His* name as their true calling, to repent, forgive and seek *His* face so that *He* can rewrite the incorrect narrative that we have willingly accepted (2 Chr 7:14).

We have erroneously received a word that siphons our hopes and aspirations and needles them down to bare necessities, instilling a poverty or lack lifestyle. But change comes when we grow in the *living and true God* and become cognizant that *He* is *Elohim*. The great *God* that created the heavens and the earth, and the fullness thereof. Acknowledging with simplicity that *He* speaks, and it is so (Matt 24:35). Upon seeking *Him* and *His* righteousness, upon seeking *His* illustrious face, upon seeking *His* voice as the *Good Shepherd*, there is a profound discovery of indescribable peace, unspeakable joy, and indefinable love that resides in the bosom of: **Jesus Christ**... **Savior**... **Messiah**... **Redeemer**... **Prince of Peace**... **Lord** of lords... **King** of kings... the perfect *Lamb of God*.

Let's not get lost and allow the desires of the world to infiltrate our hearts and minds so that we lose sight of seeking **Him** that first loved us into life on earth and promises us as believers in the **Resurrected Christ** life everlasting (1 John 4:19). Let us find the finished work that **He** has reserved for **His** sheep in seeking **El Elyon**, the completely self-existing **God**. In all of our seeking, may we find solace in **Jehovah Shalom** and fulfillment in **El Shaddai**. May our seeking **His** presence be found in worship to the **Most High**; for **He** inhabits the praises of **His** people (Psa 22:3). Draw near to **Him** who holds the answers to your every question, because as you draw near, you discover **His** proximity (James 4:8).

Our way is made prosperous and successful as we discover the jewels within the treasure trove, the *Word*; as you meditate on it day and night, that you might walk in purpose (Josh 1:8). May your appetite be satisfied not in people, places, or things such as designer clothes and accessories; not in TikTok, Instagram, Twitter, Facebook or other social media platforms that exploit your giftings… but may you be filled with an overflow that only **Jehovah Chayil**, the **God** of **Wealth** can supply; for **He** is wealth, and in **Him** there is no lack or insufficiency (Psa 34:10). Seek **Him** with your whole heart, soul and mind, and allow **Him** to quench you with **His** treasure, the *inexhaustible Word of God*.

Musings

What part of this 'Peace' stirred you and why?

_____
_____
_____
_____
_____
_____

Meanderings

Did this 'Peace' trigger any particular memory and why?

_____
_____
_____
_____
_____
_____
_____

Meditations

What secret place will you allow **Jehovah Rapha** to minister to you as you ponder this 'Peace'?

Servant

Matthew 25:21

Thy good and faithful servant... sweet, sweet words...music to the believer's ear. Words that make our heart rejoice. But faithful to whom... to what... and for what purpose? Legitimate self-evaluation. Many times, we become so involved in the service that the deceptive 'angel of light' clouds our perception of the works (2 Cor 11:14). We seek faithfulness in our study of the **Word**, study in prayer, study in fellowship with the saints. Then there is the day of exposure (Eph 5:13). What exactly were we faithful to? Better yet, who were we faithful to? Was our work in vain as we worked tirelessly in the kingdom? Sowing seeds because the **Good Shepherd** instructed us to... or did *He*? Is the seed for the edifying of the body of *Christ*? Are we sowing into the children... teaching them the **Word**... standing with them when they make mistakes, and are in the presence of administration... and in this season, the court system? How many pastors are sitting with the parent(s) as a child stands  in judgment? Are we calling the elderly in the church and making sure they have their needs met? Are the deacons standing in the gap with the widows that are left with no covering? When there is a repair that is needed in their home, are the deacons holding the repairman accountable for price gouging or faulty repairs? Just what are we being faithful to?

Church attendance... Monday night minister study... Tuesday night

Women/Men Bible Study... Wednesday night Bible study... Sunday School... Sunday Morning church service... the numerous celebrations of the officers of the church? Fellowship is practice; it's boot camp.

What are you doing when you go beyond the church doors... when you enter the real war zone? Are you willing to pull a soul out of the line of fire, or have you grown exhausted with your prayers because of disrespect and disobedience... thrown up the flag of surrender? What are you faithful over? Who are you faithful to? Are you willing to stand in the gap when there is no audience? There are no awards to give for your faithfulness... will you stand then? What you do in secret, *He* will reward openly (Matt 6:4).

Strength is service, not status. Who or what are we being good and faithful to? The *living and true God* that left instructions in *His inexhaustible Word* that cuts to the marrow... that stings, yet will not kill (2 Cor 3:6)? The *Master* said if we were faithful over a few things, we would be a ruler over many (Matt 25:23).

How many souls would be encouraged and drawn to the light of the *Most High* with more acts of selflessness outside of the studying, declaring and decreeing, and more of the actions that speak of *Jesus Christ's* selfless life (Matt 5:16)? The *Most High* searches the heart of man. *He* knows the heart of man, the deepest desires of *His* creation (Rom 8:27). Ask *Him* to give you the spirit of wisdom and revelation in the knowledge of *Him* that *He* may orchestrate your path (Eph 1:17). As you strive to complete the tasks that *He's* ordained for you, there will be no fear at the end of your journey. You will know that you will hear those desired words; there will be no doubt that you have fulfilled your reasonable service (Rom 12:1).

Glory be to the **Most High**! To hear those *Words*: Well done, Thou good and faithful servant: thou hast been faithful over a few things. ***I*** will make thee a ruler over many things: enter thou into the joy of thy ***LORD*** (Matt 25:21). Hallelujah!!!

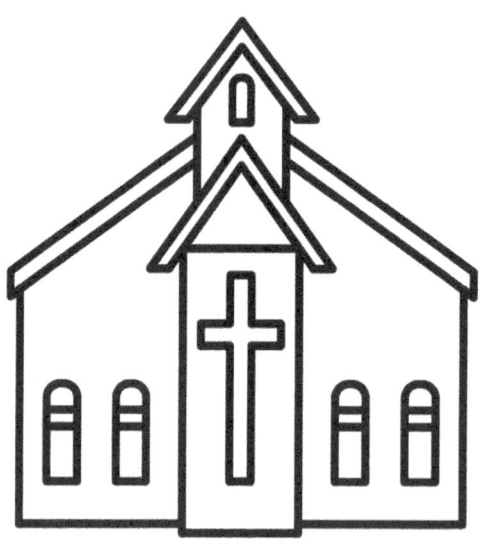

Musings

What part of this 'Peace' stirred you and why?

_____
_____
_____
_____
_____
_____

Meanderings

Did this 'Peace' trigger any particular memory and why?

_____
_____
_____
_____
_____
_____

Meditations

What secret place will you allow **Jehovah Rapha** to minister to you as you ponder this 'Peace'?

_____
_____
_____
_____
_____
_____
_____
_____
_____
_____
_____
_____
_____
_____
_____

Trust You

Proverbs 22:19

We are all looking for a hero. We're looking for that person who we can share everything with. When we make a covenant with our spouses, we expect them to be our safe place. We yield the most intimate part of ourselves to them and seek the same from them — level ground. If not a spouse or significant other, there's always that best friend. The one you grew up with or even a newfound one that you just click with.

Your experiences mirror each other's, and the vibe is seamless. There's a calm, and the more you invest in the relationship, there appears to be a few slight glitches. There are misunderstandings that are easily repaired, because we can acknowledge that we are all human, and we mess up. What happens if that relationship dissolves; where does that leave you? That person that you shared so much with abuses your confidence and your trust, taking and never wanting to give; there is no reciprocity. Remember, we wrestle not against flesh and blood, but against principalities, against power, against the rulers of the darkness of this world, against spiritual wickedness in high places (Eph 6:12). Mankind is faulty and will let you down (Psa 118:8).

There is **One** that you can trust; you can come before **Him** naked and unashamed. **He** is your hope. You have trusted **Him** from your youth.

He was consistent, even when you betrayed *Him* for a new best friend (Psa 71:5). Yep, there *He* is... where *He's* been... the entire time... with you always. *He* saw the darkest secret that you were too ashamed to tell anybody else, and *He* loved you through it. *He* forgave you when you repented, and *He* won't ever repeat it or use it as a weapon against you (1 John 1:9). *He's* the friend that sticks closer than a brother (Prov 18:24). You can trust *Him* when you can't trace *Him*. You can trust *Him* with all the many disappointments, the innumerable disillusionments, the various heartbreaks; all of your downfalls.

For *He* is the lifter up of thine head (Psa 145:14). *He* builds you up when life tenaciously and intentionally attempts to tear you down (Jude 1:20). *He* enlightens you with unveiled eyes to the attacks, the plots, the plans of 'the accuser' and gives you divine instruction for a strategic escape, ultimately your deliverance from every evil (2 Tim 4:18). *He* delivers you every day of your life. **His** love is incomparable! **His** devotion is beyond comprehension! **His** sovereign grace unmerited! **His** wisdom priceless! **His** mercy limitless! **His** plans are inconceivable! Trust the *living and true God*! Trust, **Elohim**, your **Creator**! Blessed be the **Lord God** of Israel from everlasting to everlasting! Amen and Amen (Psa 41:13).

Musings

What part of this 'Peace' stirred you and why?

_____
_____
_____
_____
_____
_____

Meanderings

Did this 'Peace' trigger any particular memory and why?

_____
_____
_____
_____
_____
_____
_____

Meditations

What secret place will you allow **Jehovah Rapha** to minister to you as you ponder this 'Peace'?

Wait

Psalm 37:7-9

I can still hear the distinctive mocking voice of Dana Dane as he cried, "Wait, wait, wait, wait!" It resonated with a lighthearted vibrancy that evoked laughter and fun. Yet how many times in the 'wait' does the weight becomes so heavy, and we grow weary in the spirit? How many times do we ask **Yahweh**, "How long, **Lord**, must I call for help, but **You** do not listen" (Hab 1:2)?

How many times do we find ourselves in dire straits as life catapults us from one catastrophic situation to another monstrosity of warfare? How many times do we view the many injustices, the unnecessary violence and cruelty; the insane malice and evil that continues to abound; and it seems as if the enemy even has the audacity to prosper and there seems to be no repercussions for the evildoer? How many?

Yahweh is the **Lord** our **God**; **His** name is a strong tower for the righteous who run to it and are safe (Prov 18:10). **He** instructs **His** sheep to be quick to hear and slow to speak; for in the meantime, between time, **He** is moving swiftly on your behalf (James 1:19). It's in the still of the moment that the **Almighty** is doing a magnificent work; it is when you are in the 'wait' that you are able to receive divine direction because you are intentional in attuning your hearing to **His** voice that you might acknowledge **Him** in all of your ways, that **He** might direct your path (Prov 3:6). That path was once rough; but

Elohim; yep, *He* did reconstructive work with *His* righteous right arm and smoothed it out for you. *He* aborted the tactics and snares of those who were adversarial (Deut 28:7).

It's in the 'wait' that you receive your beauty for ashes. It's in the 'wait' that *He* rewards you with the garment of praise for the spirit of heaviness, because the weight of it was too much to carry. It's in the 'wait' that *He* saturates you with the oil of joy in lieu of a season of mourning, and declares that the weeping was only for a night… it's morning and daybreak comes with the joy of the *Lord* (Psa 30:5; Isa 61:3)! Nothing is too hard for *God* (Jer 32:27)! *He* is the *God* of all possibilities!

Many times, we measure the 'wait' against the resolution of the circumstances; yet it's in the 'wait' that you are able to rest under the shadow of the *Almighty* (Psa 91:1). It's in the 'wait' that you witness 1,000 fall at one side and 10,000 on your right hand; yet *God* will not allow them to come near you (Psa 91:7). *He* told you that the weapons would form, but they would *not* prosper (Isa 54:17). There is purpose in the 'wait.' Because they that 'wait' upon the *Lord* shall renew their strength; they shall mount up with wings as eagles; they shall run and not be weary; and they shall walk and not faint (Isa 40:31).

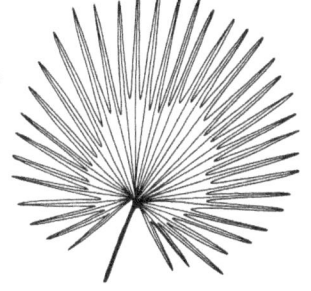

In spite of us knowing that one day with the *Lord* is as a thousand years, the 'wait' is not to discourage you, but to encourage you (2 Pet 3:8). It's in the 'wait' that you can wholeheartedly, 'Bless the *Lord* and forget not all *His* benefits.' It's in the 'wait' that *He* redeems your life from destruction. It's in the 'wait' that *He* crowns you with lovingkindness and tender mercies (Psa 103:2,4). It's in the 'wait' that you come to know *Him* as your rock, as your fortress, as your deliverer, as your strength, as your buckler, as the horn of your salvation, as your high tower (Psa 18:2)! It's in the 'wait' that you feel the *glory of God* as *He* encompasses you with *His* unconditional love!

When you find yourself in the 'wait', glorify the **Most High**! Exalt **His** majestic Name! Remember: the race is not given to the swift, nor the battle to the strong, nor bread to the wise, nor riches to men of understanding, nor favor to men of skill (Ecc 9:11). Praise **God** while you're in the 'wait'; sing unto the **Lord** a new song (Isa 42:10)! Be that warrior that will 'wait' upon the **Lord**! **He** is the 'Wait!' Let the Redeemed of the **Lord** say so (Psa 107:2)!

Musings

What part of this 'Peace' stirred you and why?

_____
_____
_____
_____
_____
_____

Meanderings

Did this 'Peace' trigger any particular memory and why?

_____
_____
_____
_____
_____
_____
_____
_____

Meditations

What secret place will you allow **Jehovah Rapha** to minister to you as you ponder this 'Peace'?

_____
_____
_____
_____
_____
_____
_____
_____
_____
_____
_____
_____
_____
_____
_____

Without You

Proverbs 22:19

Many ask that **You, Lord** don't do anything in this season without doing it with them. But for real and for true, I don't want to do 'anything' without **You**. From the rising of the sun, to the sting of the burning heat at the height of the day, to the residing redness of its glare, I find peace in **You** (Mal 1:11). The joy in calling **Your** name at 6:29 am is just as joyful as calling **Your** name at 3:18 am, and the joy is that at any time, day or night, I can call **Your** name and **You** will be there. **You're** so kind that **You** assure me that **You** answer even before I call, that **You** hear while *I am* yet speaking (Isa 65:24).

You're so mighty and strong that **You** neither slumber nor sleep (Psa 121:4). **You** are the **Eternal God** that finds joy in my weakness… being that when I am weak, I see **Your** strength (2 Cor 12:10).

Many times in life, we find ourselves on that broad path that seems to be brimming with opportunities and some unfulfilled promises. It seems to be a place where we are finally recognized for our giftings and we are celebrated… finally. If we aren't careful, we may find ourselves enamored with the accolades and the privilege that comes with being in 'your season'… until divine revelation reveals the façade for its' deceitful counterfeit activity.

What goes up must come down; that's why it's so important that we examine our hearts and our motives. If the highest

honor is to be bestowed upon you, take the time to go before the *'throne of grace'* with gratitude and humility, and seek *Abba's* face and instructions. The promises of *God* are 'yea' and 'Amen' in *Him* (Psa 55:22; 2 Cor 1:20). If *He* stamps it with *His* Word, trust that it won't return void; it shall prosper and bless you (Isa 55:11). It is *His* signet on that check; cash it, because you can rest assured that 'it is good!' *Lord God*, whatever *You're* doing in this season of my life, I don't want to do it without *You*!!!

Musings

What part of this 'Peace' stirred you and why?

_____
_____
_____
_____
_____
_____

Meanderings

Did this 'Peace' trigger any particular memory and why?

_____
_____
_____
_____
_____
_____
_____

Meditations

What secret place will you allow **Jehovah Rapha** to minister to you as you ponder this 'Peace'?

Omega Prayer

Abba Father which art in heaven, hallowed be ***Thy*** Most Holy Name! Glory be to ***You, Elohim!*** I give ***You*** the utmost honor ***O Majestic One!*** I honor ***You*** with my praise for ***You*** are ever so worthy! I exalt ***You*** in the earth as well as in the heavens! I exalt ***You*** in the land of the living all the days of my life! My lips shall continually sing ***Your*** praises! Hallelujah!

Father, we seek ***Your*** face and desire ***Your*** extraordinary peace. ***Lord God***, we pursue ***Your*** presence, ***Your*** purpose and ***Your*** pattern that will resurrect ***Your*** authentic plans for our divine purpose on earth as it is in heaven.

May the sacrifices of our joy be acceptable in ***Thy*** sight. May ***Thy*** kingdom come; may ***Thy*** will be done and magnified in this season. May ***Your*** unconditional love be translucent in "Kingdom Peaces." May the release of past hurts be humbly laid at ***Your*** feet and deliverances manifest for ***Your*** timeless glory. May lives be restored in authenticity in the divine revelation of ***Your*** healing and resurrection of bleeding souls. May the spirit of trauma, devastation and ruination be dismantled and washed afresh in the *'blood of **Jesus**.'*

May crooked paths be straightened as broken hearts are mended. May each soul that was lost be found under the *shadow of the **Almighty***, may they acknowledge ***You*** as their *place of refuge*.

May reconstruction of contrite spirits be received as a portion of ***Your*** overflow. May the sweetest aroma of ***Your*** Word be illuminated to the highest heaven. May **Your** atoning sacrifice be acknowledged, reverenced and received among the 'peaces' this day, our daily bread.

May there be a colossal indulgence in *Your undeniably majestic presence* in this ordained space of time. May the fruit of our lips be in eternal worship of **You, O Most High**. May our footsteps pattern the path of the assigned angels that prosper our way for 'kingdom' purpose.

May our daily intentions genuflect to **Your** will in our lives consistently and consciously. May the *mind of Christ* anoint, appoint, assign and design **Your** musings in our thoughts.

May **Your** uninhibited love adorn our meanderings in our testimony of overcoming by way of **Your** grace. May our fleeting time attest of meditations that magnify **Your** confirmation of our renewal in **You**. May the **Cornerstone** be edified as we are labeled as bricklayers, divine architects of the *'kingdom of heaven.'*

May the reader complete this *'vessel of exhortation'* with an astonishing awakening of uncommon grace from the last page to the first. May there be an irrevocable fresh oil anointing the reader for **Your** *glory* alone.

May the cup that **You** predestined for **Your** children overflow with **Your Word**, **Your** blessings and **Your** glory, **O Most High**.

May the reader gracefully take their seat at **Your** prepared table and feast on the *bread of heaven*. May they be revived as an heir of the **Most High** and never accept the crumbs again.

May they honor the *blessings of Abraham* over their lives and their descendants in humility and grace; believing that **YESHUA** qualifies them.

May "Kingdom Peaces" be acceptable as a living sacrifice placed before **Your** *'throne of grace.'*

May **You** be elevated in the earth realm as in the heavenlies.

May the edification of **Your Word** that saturates "Kingdom Peaces" reside in the archives of heaven to be sung among the heavenly hosts that worship **You** from everlasting to everlasting.

May **El Shaddai** bless this work and pour immeasurable blessings upon "Kingdom Peaces."

Now **Elohim**, the *Mighty Majestic* **Creator**, may this *'vessel of worship'* be acceptable in **Your** sight. I pray that these humble "Kingdom Peaces" bring **You** eternal glory. I speak it; therefore I believe it is sealed with the *blood of the slain* **Lamb of God**.

Glory Hallelujah! I humbly seal this prayer in the *inexhaustible name of* **Jesus**, my **Saviour**, my **Redeemer**, my **Deliverer**, Your **Eternal Word**! Amen!

Author's Page

Author Tamela Winfrey is a lover of the Word of **God**. She is a devout Woman of **God** and a Kingdom Builder. She is the mother of two (2) beloved children. She is a faithful daughter to her cherished parents. She is a loyal sister and friend that loves with her whole heart. She has worked in the field of finance for 30+ years. She is an avid reader and is a diligent seeker of gemstones within each new read. Tamela is an affirmed book reviewer. She loves encouraging and promoting authors and witnessing the greatness that resides within the pages of each new creation. She is an editor and has no inhibition in sharing her ideas and assisting in building another's vision for their projects.

Tamela is unorthodox in her thoughts and creativity, for she intentionally seeks to diligently provoke the *'voice'* of the **Most High** in all of her assignments. She has been writing what she deems as 'peaces' for years. "Kingdom Peaces" is the birthing of her first published spiritual baby and it shall not be the last. Tamela desires to 'tell the story' many think, but never utter. To speak of the forgotten, the overlooked, the misfits, the misused, to speak a truth that is uncomfortable, yet bears relevance and is authentically significant. To give volume, light and liberation to those held captive by their surroundings and their experiences of hurt, disillusionment and trauma. "Kingdom Peaces" will give amplified voice to those who only whisper because of intimidation and the misunderstanding of who they are and to WHOM they belong. Tamela's love for **Elohim** is the overshadowing of her walk and the essence of who she strives to be in her talk. If you ask her, 'Who is Tamela L. Winfrey?' Her reply is: I am just Tammye, a devoted student of **Christ**.